THROUGH THE BOMBSIGHT

Through the Bombsight

Squadron Leader
ANDREW MAITLAND
DFC and Bar

WILLIAM KIMBER · LONDON

First published in 1986 by
WILLIAM KIMBER & CO LIMITED
100 Jermyn Street, London, SW1Y 6EE

© Andrew Maitland, 1986
ISBN 0-7183-0620-1

Typeset by Spire Print Services Limited,
Salisbury, Wiltshire
Printed in Great Britain by
Redwood Burn Limited, Trowbridge, Wiltshire

For Roy

Who I know greatly admires the spirit and courage of the
wartime aircrew of the Royal Air Force

Contents

List of Illustrations

The author and publishers would like to thank Mr Chaz Bowyer for his advice on, and provision of, photographs for this book.

Foreword

Bomber Command of the Royal Air Force was to play a very large and important part in the defeat of the Third Reich. The aircrew who manned the bombers were all volunteers and came from Britain, the Commonwealth and Empire and other Allied Air Forces and were probably the best educated and most highly trained officers and NCOs to have fought in the front line of any war.

They never flinched from carrying out their tour of duty against sometimes the most frightening and terrible defences that left little scope for survival. No men in the history of warfare have ever been asked to embark upon so many deadly and dangerous operations, every one of them a separate battle with the odds very much stacked against them. It is not surprising that the hostile skies of Germany were to claim over 47,000 aircrew killed in the many sorties carried out against the enemy's towns and cities and the thousands of other targets of importance to the Third Reich.

At various stages of the bombing offensive aircrew would have little chance of completing a tour of 30 operations and at the worst times on the operational squadrons, many did not expect to complete a tour. They were all brave, courageous young men who wholeheartedly believed that the contribution that the bombers were making was a very much worthwhile one, especially in the years between Dunkirk and the opening of the Second Front when the bombers were the only means of attacking the German homeland.

Since the end of the Second World War historians have had

varying views on the achievements of the bomber offensive. Some have been most critical while others have been more complimentary and I believe some have changed their minds over the 40 years since the end of the war. Some will argue that the cost in lives and money was far too great a price to pay for the Command's achievements, but this is difficult to assess when one thinks of the many thousands of lives that must have been saved when the Allied armies burst out of Normandy and had a fairly easy advance into Germany. One asks would this have been possible with so few casualties without the bomber offensive? Would the German economy which was in ruins by the end of March 1945 have lasted longer if there had been no bombing offensive?

During the war I was to spend about fifteen months altogether as a bomb aimer on Bomber Command operational squadrons and was extremely fortunate to survive 74 operational sorties in various roles as shown in Appendix A. I have endeavoured to write in this book my own experiences, my own views and my own thoughts while serving as a member of aircrew on Bomber Command.

I am very proud to have served with such brave young men in that Command and will forever remember those who fell in battle and think of them as some of the cream of my generation.

CHAPTER I

Early Years and Enlistment

'They have sown the wind, they will reap the whirlwind.' Words spoken by one of the greatest wartime commanders when early in the Second World War the German Luftwaffe started bombing the centres of population in Great Britain.

The commander was none other than Marshal of The Royal Air Force, Sir Arthur Harris, the wartime Commander-in-Chief of RAF Bomber Command. Harris was affectionally known as 'Butch' by all who served in the many squadrons and units of that great Command. He was a great leader of a Command that was to contribute so much to the war effort and was a man completely dedicated to the destruction by area bombing of the German war industries which were so vital to the supply of war materials necessary for the German armed forces to continue waging war.

There can be little doubt that one of the greatest contributing factors in the defeat of Nazi Germany and their mighty war machine was the strategic bombing offensive carried out by the Royal Air Force against German factories, workshops, military installations, fuel supplies, communications, and many other targets necessary to the Germans in waging war. The sustained attacks carried out night after night by the heavy bombers on the German industrial heartland was in the end to play a vital part in the inability of the German armed forces to continue waging war. Although it has been claimed by some historians that mass bombing did not break the morale of the German civilian population, it must have strained it to the utmost limits.

The Battle of Britain had been fought during the summer of

1940 and by October that year a glorious victory had been won, not without sacrifice, by the men of RAF Fighter Command. The victory not only cheered the hearts of the British people in these islands, but all other freedom-loving folks throughout the world.

The German war machine that had conquered and subjugated most of the countries of Europe had been halted and received its first major defeat since Hitler came to power. Before attempting a landing by seaborne and airborne forces on the British mainland the enemy required air supremacy over Britain and to achieve this they dispatched their bomber force in hundreds against the south of England in an all out effort to drive the RAF fighter aircraft from the skies. The battle raged as Spitfire and Hurricane fighters met the bomber stream and although heavily outnumbered they took such a toll of the enemy bombers that by the end of September 1940 the Germans broke off their daytime bombing and the RAF still reigned supreme over the British Isles. So outnumbered were the fighter squadrons involved in the battle and so glorious the victory won by the RAF fighter pilots, that Winston Churchill praised them in these words: 'Never in the field of human conflict was so much owed by so many to so few.'

The victory by the 'Few' was a tremendous morale booster for the whole British nation as they had up to then very little to enthuse about since the start of the war. The threat of invasion which had haunted them since the army's retreat from Dunkirk had been lifted from their minds and a new spirit was abroad in the country and although Britain stood alone against the mightiest war machine the world had ever seen, they were not interested in defeat as that possibility did not exist in their minds. Their objective was the total defeat of the Nazi hordes who were cruelly subjugating most of Europe. There would be no let-up till final victory was achieved even though the road might be long and hard.

By the end of 1940 British industry had moved on to a complete war footing and the weapons of war were rolling off the assembly lines at an ever increasing rate and the fighting forces

Air Chief Marshal Sir Arthur Harris, KCB, OBE, AFC – AOC-in-C, Bomber Command 1942–5

could look forward to more and better weapons for the battles that lay ahead.

Aid was beginning to arrive from friendly countries beyond the seas. The Royal Navy and British Merchant Service were doing a magnificent job on the high seas which were alive with German U-boats and although the merchant fleet was taking heavy losses a great tonnage of vital supplies was reaching British seaports.

It was quite obvious to Mr Churchill and the British war leaders that while training of personnel and the build-up of war materials was in progress it would be necessary to strike at the enemy by all means at their disposal to try and weaken the German fortress of Europe before dispatching an invasion fleet to tackle a landing. The obvious weapon, in fact the only weapon available to strike at the heartland of Germany and their defences in Europe, was the bomber; so the day of the bomber had arrived.

By 1941 the British Government was committed to building a large bomber force for the RAF and this was beginning to take shape, not an easy task considering the bombers were highly technical machines requiring high technical skills from the workers in the aircraft industry, many of whom were newcomers to plane making. The other big problem facing the Government in forming the bombing force was that a very large number of trained aircrew would be required to man these sophisticated bombers. Fortunately a scheme had been worked out with the Commonwealth and the United States of America to train aircrew for the RAF and this was to be a trump card in our war effort. Crews were trained in the USA, Canada, South Africa and Rhodesia.

I, as an aircrew cadet, was to be trained in the United States and Canada.

*

Prior to my enlistment in the Royal Air Force in 1941, I had been employed by Scottish Aviation at Prestwick Aerodrome, now the Scottish International Airport of Prestwick. Before the war and in the early years of the war, the airfield had a grass surface with no runways, but this was adequate for the Elementary Flying Training School with Tiger Moths and The Observer School with Anson Aircraft. These training schools were training pilots and observers for the RAF.

My post with Scottish Aviation was that of clerk in the Watch Office or Time Office which was a forerunner of Air Traffic Control. The office was responsible for the booking in and out of aircraft and their crews and the recording of all flying times and air exercises carried out by aircrew. I had taken the position at Prestwick because of my love of flying and had hoped, pre-war, to join the Auxiliary Air Force (the Weekend Flyers). When the war came along I very much wanted to get into the RAF but being at Prestwick I was in a reserved occupation, which interfered with my plans and it was not until 1941 I was able to escape from my tied job.

In April 1941 I found that provided I volunteered for aircrew duties and was accepted by the RAF I could be released from my reserved occupation. I was off to the recruiting centre at St Mungo's Halls in Glasgow where I duly volunteered, had a preliminary medical, a small academic examination, an interview and a promise that my name would be submitted to the Air Crew Selection Centre in Edinburgh and they would decide whether or not to call me for a full aircrew selection.

I had to wait some three weeks before being called to the Selection Centre for the three day selection procedure that meant so much to me and my future career. The first day of selection was spent in background details and a very full and exacting aircrew medical. Second day was spent mainly in the classroom and the third day I appeared before a selection board made up of several fairly high-ranking officers. The senior member of the board was an air commodore, who made it quite clear to me that they not only wanted people to learn to fly, but men who could be taught to fly and fight in the air. My interview must have lasted about fifteen minutes and many and varied were the questions I was posed, from background to schooling to general knowledge, all designed to find out if the candidate had

15

the ability and the desire to become a member of aircrew in the Royal Air Force. At the end of my interview I was asked to wait in an adjoining room.

After I had waited about ten minutes or so, which seemed to me an eternity, an NCO clerk appeared at the door and called my name. I answered smartly and he handed me a piece of paper which had my name on it, informing me I had been selected for training as pilot or observer and I was to return to my home and await my call up for training.

I heaved a sigh of relief and was overjoyed that at least I was going to be given the opportunity of making the grade as aircrew and that I would not have to spend the remainder of the war at Prestwick tied to a desk in the Time Office.

Before leaving the Selection Centre I was to find that of some forty candidates appearing for the three day selection, only about nine had qualified for aircrew training, so I felt pleased I had been fortunate enough to make the grade which I considered a fairly high standard, considering the country was at war and losses of aircrew could be expected to increase as the number of aircraft available become greater.

I returned home and continued with my employment as I anxiously awaited my call to full time service. My call up was to come at the beginning of July 1941 and instructed me to report to RAF Babbacombe near Torquay on 9th July. The main function of this unit, which was an aircrew receiving centre, was to fit us out with uniforms, flying kit and all the other bits and pieces of equipment required by the modern airman. Our inoculations and vaccinations were brought up to date. We were introduced to RAF drill and the drill sergeant, physical training and cross country runs. We were lectured on maintenance and kit lay-out, Air Force law, medical and hygiene and many other odds and ends that would get us started on the road to becoming efficient aircrew cadets.

Fortunately the weather was bright, warm and sunny during our week's stay at Babbacombe and I enjoyed it tremendously. My feet were a bit sore breaking in new boots on a drill square, but the swimming in the evenings helped to relieve the agony along with a couple of pints of scrumpy cider at the local bar which was guaranteed to kill the pain. It was about 20th July that we had to say our fond farewell to beautiful Babbacombe with its lovely beach and warm weather, and board a special train for our journey to our Initial Training School at Scarborough in Yorkshire.

At Scarborough we were to be licked into shape both physically and mentally in preparation for flying training. A great number of hours during our eight weeks at ITW were to be spent drilling with and without rifles along the Scarborough promenade. Physical training was carried out on the sand and route marches and cross crountry runs, up and down the steepest hills in town. When we were not marching or running we were being instructed in maths, navigation, meteorology, theory of flight, aircraft engines, Air Force law and some other bits and pieces associated with flying. Each instructor was a specialist in his own particular subject and there was no excuse why interested students should not learn rapidly from their teachings.

Our particular classroom had been a restaurant and coffee bar at the south end front of the Grand Hotel where I was lucky enough to be quartered. It was mainly of glass observation windows, well ventilated, giving a good view of the promenade and North Sea, not that we got much time to admire the view as our instruction was fast and furious. In the early days of ITW, like many of the others, I was to feel tired with the physical and mental exertions of the daily routine, but as time passed and we became fitter we felt less tired and managed to get out in the evenings and refresh ourselves in the local pubs. I don't remember beer tasting so good.

The social highlight of our week was a cadet dance held in the Royal Hotel just round the corner from the Grand. The dance was always well attended by the young ladies of the town and I think the surrounding countryside. It was a pleasant change from male company. There always seemed to be sufficient food and drink to keep most people happy which was quite amazing when one remembered how strictly food was rationed. The dance was a great way to relax and get away for a short time from our very exacting routine.

There was one snag with our Saturday night dance and that was when we had to rise on Sunday morning and prepare for the Church parade. We marched about a mile to Church on Sunday so by the time we got there our heads were clear and we were in better shape for hymn singing. Fortunately after Church service the remainder of the day was free but like many of my colleagues, I spent the time on private study and writing up notes from our week's lectures. As we neared the end of our ITW course the time had arrived for the inevitable examinations and of course this involved a certain amount of revision on examination subjects. There was always the threat that any cadet not reaching the required standard would be suspended from the Aircrew Course, so these examinations had to be taken seriously.

When the examinations were over I felt they had been very fair and I think most candidates thought the same, although there were a few failures. By the time the exams were behind us, rumours were rife that cadets gaining the best marks were to be trained in the USA, so the thought of visiting the States was one which I savoured.

On completion of the ITW course, a few well-earned days' leave was appreciated.

CHAPTER II

United States 1941

On arrival back at the Grand Hotel I was instructed to visit the clothing store and be issued with a light grey flannel suit and several other civilian garments. Although I had not been told that I was on my way to the United States it was now becoming pretty obvious where I was going to be trained, as International Law would not allow us to wear uniforms in the States as they were still at peace, hence the civilian garments.

A few more days at Scarborough and it was off by train to an overseas embarkation centre at Wilmslow, Cheshire to await passage by ship to Canada.

Wilmslow was a typical embarkation unit, being overcrowded, not very clean and with very mediocre food. I was therefore quite delighted to move out after only a few days to be taken to the docks at Liverpool to embark on *The Highland Princess*, a medium-sized passenger cargo ship converted for troop-carrying. This ship was on the Argentina/United Kingdom run pre-war and one of the wags in our company was not slow to put it around that our mess deck which was to be our home for the next week or so was where they used to store the frozen meat enroute from South America to UK.

We set sail from Liverpool on 30th September and I remember thinking that should we be torpedoed I didn't hold out much hope of escape. However one did not think these things out loud and tried to put them to the back of one's mind. We settled in our new abode and the morale and spirits seemed to be high considering the very cramped conditions. The food, although not Cordon Bleu, was good, wholesome stuff and one

19

had no reason to go hungry. I was not interested in food for the first couple of days at sea as I spent my time looking green and felt a little sick trying to get my sea legs – pity because 1st October was my birthday. Once I got over these first two days I was a great sailor. I have always been the same on my first two days at sea. I must be like Lord Nelson who was always sick his first two days at sea.

On the first few days of the voyage I calculated we had made our way from Liverpool up the Irish Sea and out into the Atlantic through the approaches between Northern Ireland and the Mull of Kintyre. On this part of the journey we were accompanied by about seven destroyers or frigates, two more troopships and several more assorted cargo ships. All this in one convoy. I woke on the morning of the third day out to find that we were alone with an escort of one destroyer and one armed merchantman so only hoped that this would be enough to see us across a hostile Atlantic. On the early afternoon of the third day while sailing in quite calm water and a fairly clear sky, the alarm bells sounded Action Stations and we hurried to our allocated boat station. A Fokke Wolf Kurier could be clearly seen appearing from time to time over the horizon to the rear of our ship. Both the destroyer and armed merchantman closed in behind us and several rounds of anti-aircraft shells were fired at the intruder who did not appear too keen to come any closer to the ship, so one could only assume that he was on a spotting mission for German U-boats in the area. I felt during the hours of darkness on that night many alterations of course were made to outwit any submarines that might be lurking in that part of the ocean that had been reconnoitred by the German aircraft.

The Highland Princess docked in Halifax on the afternoon of 9th October, but it was about ten o'clock that night before we were to disembark and take our seats on the special train drawn up in the dockside station and destined to carry us to Toronto.

A train journey from Halifax to Toronto in early October is something to behold and savour. The trees were so wonderful and each one more beautiful than the other with autumn leaves in so many glorious colours. This real feast of scenic beauty reminded me so much of the Scottish Highlands during the autumn months. As I sat there in the window seat absorbed in the beauty of the view, the train rumbled on revealing more and more of this vast land.

Soon we were speeding along the banks of the St Lawrence and then on to Levis to look over the river to Quebec standing above the Heights of Abraham. Stopping at Levis to refuel, the City of Quebec seemed to stand there majestically looking down upon us. This type of journey, at least to me, seemed to have no dull moments; if it was not the forests, lakes and towns, there was the wild life. I remember seeing beavers working on their dam. On nearing Toronto I was sorry the journey was coming to an end, for seldom if ever, had I experienced such a pleasant, beautiful journey.

No one seemed quite sure how long we would be in Toronto before moving to the United States. I don't think anyone was in too big a hurry to move as the Canadian people were overwhelming with their hospitality and many were the social invitations that we received. The first Sunday in Toronto the city councillors decided they would take a group of cadets on a visit to Niagara Falls. As only a limited number could join this group a draw was held to pick the lucky names, so lucky me – my name came out of the hat.

One of the councillors and his wife picked up myself and another cadet early on Sunday morning and we were on our way in a very comfortable motor car. On the first stage of our journey we stopped for lunch at an orchard farm near Hamilton where a very nice lunch had been arranged in the orchards where magnificent red, rosy apples were hanging in abundance on the many trees. Having thanked our hosts it was then on to Niagara to view the Falls and walk round the town and in the early evening enjoy a wonderful dinner in a nice hotel overlooking the Falls which had been illuminated as darkness fell. I will always remember that wonderful day and the kind, kind folk who made it such a memorable occasion for us British cadets.

Toronto to me was a great city and seemed so very British with so many English and Scots about who were so kind to us.

21

On 16th October 1941, we boarded the reserved coaches of a train for our journey to Montgomery, Alabama.

The sun was shining and outside the weather looked glorious as we steamed on towards Montgomery and I feasted my eyes on the beauty of the Southern States. It was around lunch time when our train pulled in to the rail siding at the United States Army Air Force Base at Maxwell Field, Montgomery. This was to be our base for the next few weeks where we would become acclimatized and carry out an American Initial Training Course very similar in lots of ways to the Initial Training Wing Course we had completed at Scarborough.

The base at Maxwell was a modern, well run establishment with good living quarters and a good Mess Hall serving excellent food. There were quite a number of grass fields on the base and the facilities for recreation and sport were excellent and their use encouraged. The classrooms and academic facilities were of the best and the instructors were most patient and helpful.

The life at Maxwell was not easy but most cadets did not mind as they were all very fit from the ITW Course in England. Some British cadets objected to having to learn American rifle drill after our course of RAF drill at ITW. The grievances were soon overcome as the British squadrons competed with the American squadrons for a special pennant which was awarded to the best squadron on parade each day. The British were most successful in the daily competition as their long arm swing while on the march seemed to impress those judging the squadron performances. One little niggle that UK cadets seemed to harbour was not being able to leave the Post after working hours during week days. Leave from Maxwell was limited to one o'clock on Saturday afternoon till two on Sunday afternoon and this was curtailed if one had incurred more than ten demerits during the week. This meant an hour's walk on the square on Saturday afternoon. The answer was to try and avoid demerits which were awarded on things like room tidiness, kit layout, smartness on parade, and many other small infringements of the Discipline Code. I was fortunate in not incurring more than the permitted misdemeanours and was set free on Saturday afternoons.

I was most impressed with the calibre of the American cadet I met at Maxwell. They certainly appeared to have been very well selected for the job. The majority were polite, well mannered, well disciplined, clean cut, athletic young men and it was so wonderful to see such healthy competition between the RAF and US cadets. Like all cadets at Maxwell I was issued with the US Army Air Corp Cadet Handbook – quite a book with hundreds of pages and thousands of words of advice and instruction in what was expected from cadets. Every cadet was expected to read this book thoroughly and ensure he understood the standards that were expected from a future officer, especially in the fields of discipline, manners and bearing.

The public crowded on to the base on Sunday afternoons when they were invited to watch the drill competition between the various squadrons. I remember one US officer would tell us that it was the RAF they were coming to see and not the Americans. However both RAF and US cadets always appeared to give of their best and the public enjoyed every minute of this very impressive performance of foot and rifle drill.

During my stay at Montgomery the weather was warm and sunny with clear blue skies and with a bonus like this life is made a little easier. One or two little incidents seem to stick in one's mind about stations or units and in the case of Maxwell Field I remember when I was given a crewcut and could not believe my eyes when I looked in the mirror; never had I seen my hair so short before or since. Then there was the day on the sports field playing volley ball and the voice of my instructor filled my ear with, 'Hey there mister, let's not kick the volley ball.' The occasion in the dining hall when I saw a US cadet being punished by having to eat a square meal because of some misdemeanour while at dinner. It certainly seemed a very uncomfortable way in which to have to take one's food and did not think he would be keen to have a repeat performance.

There is little doubt that the course for British and US cadets at Maxwell was of a high standard both in discipline and all other forms of training and most certainly compared favourably with the RAF Initial Training School Course which we had undergone in the United Kingdom.

23

With one Initial Training complete it was time to say a fond farewell to Maxwell Field and Montgomery and to move to our Primary Training Schools to start our Elementary Flying Training and in my case, it was training at Southern Aviation School, Camden, South Carolina.

Southern Aviation Field was a very compact little set-up with barracks, mess hall, classrooms all clustered together and the hangers, airfield and aircraft quite close by. The airfield had a grass surface, not too big but big enough for the Sterman Primary Trainer Aircraft which we would be using. The Sterman was a single engine biplane with two open cockpits and very similar to the Tiger Moth used at Elementary Flying Training Schools in the UK. A very light aircraft with a metal frame and fabric covering with the usual controls and basic instruments and to look at it seemed a fairly simple machine to fly.

The training programme was designed to give us alternate days on flying and ground school and with private study in the evenings. There were no pass outs in the evenings during the week days but we had Saturday and Sunday free. This set up I didn't mind as I was keen to get on with the course. At the weekends some of the American cadets with cars showed us the countryside and we visited cities like Columbia and Charlotte in North Carolina. These cadets always ensured we were well entertained at parties and dances and this gave us a great opportunity to meet many American families who were always most kind and hospitable and believe me this hospitality was greatly appreciated as the $22 a fortnight we were paid did not stretch too far and a couple of nights out in town took care of our meagre salary. I was thoroughly enjoying my stay at Camden and I was savouring my flying in Stermans and seemed to be making good progress in my ground school studies.

I did know from various sources, but mainly from other cadets, that the elimination rate for pilots training in the Arnold Scheme was very high and it was rumoured that only about 10% would succeed in completing primary training school. However this did not worry me as I was fairly confident I could make the grade and go solo after ten hours' dual instruction. However we were not to be allowed ten hours' flying to solo.

Mr Grubb, my instructor, was quite pleased with my progress and after 7 hours 50 minutes flying I was given a test by a Mr Pollock and a couple of days later I was tested by a Mr Hunter with whom I was not particularly enamoured as his instructions were shouted at the top of his voice over the aircraft intercommunication system. However after this rather harassing experience I had done all that had been asked of me and I was still convinced I could fly the aeroplane solo.

The next flying day was 29th November 1941, and well I remember it as I was to be checked by the US Army Check Pilot. Even at this stage I was not afraid of being suspended as I felt I could pass the test. The test took about 45 minutes and at the end of it much to my amazement, the Check Pilot informed me I would be suspended from flying training as a pilot. I felt like bursting out crying, but I kept a stiff upper lip and enquired why I could not have a few more hours to solo. His reply was one of sympathy, but I did not want sympathy I wanted a few more hours' flying. However much I pleaded he stood firm about his decision and I was suspended.

My whole world seemed to have fallen about me as I made my way to the instructors' room to report to my instructor Mr Grubb who appeared to think I should not have been eliminated and suggested I have another talk with the Army Check Pilot. However when I tried to see him he had disappeared and I felt perhaps I had argued with him enough, so I was just going to have to accept his findings, but it was not easy and I think I was more angry at the fact that I had come such a long way and they were not prepared to let me have a few more hours to solo. It was a sad day for me, but the American and RAF cadets, some already suspended, were most sympathetic so it helped to soften the blow.

The next day I was interviewed by the RAF Liaison Officer at Camden, Flight Lieutenant Taggart, and I let him know my feelings about the whole affair, but I got the impression he had heard all this stuff before and although he was most sympathetic, he was not in a position to reverse the Army Check Pilot's decision. He informed me that I had been recommended for observer training and that I would have a Reselection Board in Canada. The night before I was due to start my journey to Canada I busied myself packing my kit, but still felt sad and disillusioned and was more than a little angry that I had not been given a little bit more of an opportunity to prove my ability.

Even in this what I considered the first great failure of my life, I kept recalling a great saying of my mother's which was, 'Remember when one door closes, two more will open.'

CHAPTER III

Canada 1942

I reached New Brunswick in December to find Moncton gripped in the cold of the Canadian winter and very much snow-bound. This Royal Air Force Station was not to be one of my favourite units as there was not a great lot to take up one's time except clear snow, parade and hang around awaiting the Reselection Board. I did try to use some of my time in studying some of the subjects I would come up against on the observer course. When I escaped to the town of Moncton after working hours it was to the outside skating rinks that I made my way.

It was shortly after the New Year 1942 that I was to appear before a Selection Board and be reselected for observer training after trying to convince the board members that I thought if given another opportunity on a pilot's course I could make the grade. However I got the distinct impression that many of the cadets returning from the USA for reselection were feeling the same as myself, so for me it was no further pilot training, but reselected for observer training.

At the end of the second week in January I was on my way by train to No 7 Air Observer School at Portage La Prairie, Manitoba, roughly about halfway across Canada and about 30 miles due west of Winnipeg.

The Canadian Air Force Station No 7 Air Observer School was a few miles from the town of Portage La Prairie, but one got the impression it was miles from the nearest civilisation. The buildings were of wooden construction and were kept fairly warm with central heating keeping the inside temperatures up in the sixties. The weather conditions were very, very cold and we

Anson of 33 SFTS, Carberry, Manitoba, in early 1943 on a cross-country flight.

Bristol Bolinbroke, 9161, trainer in Canada. Note the black and yellow striping.

often had snow blizzards and would find ourselves digging a way out of our quarters after a night's snowfall.

The Anson aircraft we were flying were not the warmest of aircraft for this type of climate. The day flying was quite bearable as we often had good days with sunshine and good visibility. Night flying could often be quite hazardous and frequent snow showers would reduce visibility making it difficult to pick up ground objects and often would black out lights at airfields which were often the selected turning points on our cross country exercises. One of the greatest aids to air navigation over the Prairies in winter was the railway tracks. As they were always kept clear and showed up well in the white wilderness they were a great comfort to a navigator when no other pinpoints were available. If one got lost then by flying low and reading a station name the problem was solved, but no doubt frowned upon by navigation instructors. My biggest problem in navigating was cold hands, but I became very adept at drawing lines on a chart and keeping a navigation log with fingers covered in two pairs of gloves.

It was not surprising during my time at Portage I suffered two attacks of flu as the temperatures were so different from the heat of the southern states of the USA. I did not rate 7 Air Observer School, Portage La Prairie, one of my favourite stations as I never felt very comfortable in the severe cold outdoors. It was just as well that we had an enormous amount of classroom work to get through as the rooms were always at a reasonable temperature which gave good working conditions.

My visits to Portage town were quite infrequent as there was very little entertainment outside the local bowling alley which for most of the time was overcrowded. I visited an ice hockey match held in a corrugated barn type building, but although wrapped up well, I still felt very cold and had to leave before the finish.

The highlights of my stay at Portage was to escape to Winnipeg on a 48 hour pass when I would visit friends of my folks who had come to Winnipeg from Scotland some 30 years earlier. This to me was a home from home and the Ritchies, God bless them, made my weekends in Winnipeg. Old Bob Ritchie would often wait up late if I had been to a party or dance and greet me with a whisky when I returned and then we would sit talking mainly about Scotland and the town of Ayr into the small hours of the morning. I was always sorry when I had to leave the Ritchie's home and return to Portage as they always treated me like one of the family.

I cannot honestly say I was sorry to say goodbye to Portage as the only thing I would remember it for was the hard work and the bitter cold weather. Perhaps I would have appreciated the place more if I had been there during the summer months.

On leaving Portage I was granted two weeks' leave before having to report to my next unit at Mountain View, Ontario. One of my instructors at Portage by the name of Al Ekert was to invite me for a week's holiday at his parent's farm at Seaforth, Ontario, and I was to accept his offer. The weather was good and my week's stay on the farm was so relaxing and also entertaining as Al's brother and sisters did everything in their power to see that every minute of my time was usefully employed. If it was not motoring around seeing the countryside, it was meeting their friends or attending barn dances which were great fun in this part of the world and very much like Scottish country dancing. The week seemed to go in all too quickly and it was time to say goodbye and make my way by train to Toronto and then on to Bellville which was the rail station for the RCAF station at Mountain View. Mountain View was only a short distance from Bellville and was quite near Lake Ontario. It was a bombing and gunnery school and this was where I was to start my course in bombing as the observer course had now been split into navigator and air bomber categories and I was to train as an air bomber.

This type of flying appealed to me very much and I enjoyed the practice bombing exercises which consisted of dropping 10lb practice bombs on a target set up in the waters of Lake Ontario. Our bomb bursts were plotted by manned observation towers on the shore and they were able to give us the results we achieved in our bombing from about 10,000 feet. It was quite amazing how accurate one became after a few practice bombing exercises with the Mk IX bombsight. I preferred bombing from Ansons rather than Fairey Battles which were old and tended to take in lots of exhaust smoke when the clear vision panel under the bombsight was opened up. This glass panel on the underfuselage of the aircraft was pulled back to give the bomb aimer an unrestricted view of the ground through the bombsight. Unfortunately this smoke tended to distract one's concentration and too much of it could be quite sickening.

The Anson seemed a much stabler platform for bombing and also gave the bomb aimer in the nose better all round vision on his bombing run. The air photograph was usually taken from the free gun position at the rear of the pilot's position on Fairey Battles. The exercises consisted of navigating to some place, building or object and taking pictures of the subject with a handheld Mk XXIV camera and much to my surprise these pictures usually turned out very sharp and clear.

I was now enjoying my flying, having now run into much warmer and clearer weather conditions and was enjoying the Ontario scenery especially around Lake Ontario where a large number of small islands made it all look so beautiful.

At this stage of my training I was beginning to long for the day I could get back to the United Kingdom and contribute something towards the war effort. One tended to forget that this was what our training was all designed for as we were such a long way from the front line. It was with thoughts like that in my mind that I was quite pleased to complete the course at Mountain View which had been much more pleasant than my winter on the Prairies.

My next move was to my final phase of training in Canada and was to the Air Bomber Navigation Course at No 10 Air Observer School at Chatham, New Brunswick, where we arrived at the beginning of September 1942.

Chatham was a very pleasant RCAF station on the coast looking across to Prince Edward Island and during my six weeks here the training was fast and furious and included map reading, navigation, reconnaissance, signals, photography, bombing, but the weather was kind to us and I enjoyed every minute of my stay. Even with all this concentration of work I managed a few games of golf and also managed a small party with a few of my pals to celebrate my twenty-first birthday. Perhaps I did drink a bit too much on that occasion, but one is only twenty-one once.

CHAPTER IV

Lossiemouth and Rufforth

I well remember that day in October 1942, a few days after my twenty-first birthday, parading at RCAF station Chatham, New Brunswick, to be presented with my Flying Badge and to join that elite force known as aircrew in the Royal Air Force. I was proud to belong to this band of men, every one a volunteer for aircrew duties. Men who had been specially selected and had come from all walks of life and had undergone the most rigorous and exacting training to equip them to fly and fight in the air, to defend our island home and carry the fight to the enemy.

The air bomber at this time was a completely new aircrew category as prior to the the Royal Air Force trained observers who were both navigators and bomb aimers, but due to the complexity of the modern bomber it became necessary to split the observer category into separate categories of navigator and air bomber.

From all the training I had received in Canada it was quite obvious to me that the air bomber and navigator would work together as a closely knit team when in operations on heavy bombers.

I returned to the United Kingdom just before Christmas 1942, having crossed the Atlantic on the *Queen Elizabeth*, a splendid voyage with no bad weather and no apparent U-boat interference and taking only about five days from Halifax to the Clyde. We disembarked at Greenock and were transported by special train to Panel Ash College at Harrogate, Yorkshire, where, after a couple of days of documentation and kitting, we were granted leave and I was off like a shot to Scotland to spend

Christmas with my folks with instructions to report to Operational Training Unit (OTU) RAF Lossiemouth on 27th December 1942.

I spent a happy Christmas with my family and it never ceased to amaze me how the old folks managed to ensure that they had sufficient food ration coupons to provide an excellent Christmas dinner. I managed a couple of games of golf, quite a feat considering the weather. Next to flying this was my first love, as prior to enlisting I was a 6 handicap player, so I only hoped that perhaps when I got some spare time I could keep getting some practice from time to time.

My leave seemed to go all too quickly and on 27th December as instructed I was booking in at RAF Lossiemouth. The small village of Lossiemouth lies on the east coast of Scotland between Aberdeen and Inverness. A beautiful little place looking so peaceful with its small harbour and its small fishing fleet tied up alongside. This was certainly one of the most quiet and peaceful little places in the British Isles in which one could carry out Operational Flying Training.

The airfield was right on the coast, only a short distance away from the small harbour. Along the outer perimeter fence between the airfield and the sea lay a very fine golf course much to my delight, but unfortunately as it turned out, I was kept so busy I only managed a couple of rounds. However that kept my hand in and I was not complaining.

Twenty Operational Training Unit was equipped with Wellington aircraft, many of them having seen better days and a little bit worse off for wear. This was not surprising as many of them probably had seen operational duty against the enemy as Wellingtons were amongst the first of our bombers to attack Germany. On close examination I thought how frail the fabric looked that covered the criss-cross geodetic metal construction that made up the fuselage of the aircraft. However what was most important was that the two very fine Pegasus XVIII engines were kept in good running order and well maintained and serviced, so as to keep turning while airborne. If this could be relied on then we had a good chance of completing the course.

34

Our first priority on starting the OTU course was to sort ourselves into crews and this was most important as we would stay with our selected crews for the remainder of our training and for our first tour of operations against the enemy. One can well understand it was very necessary to crew with men who as far as possible had similar interests and were likely to work well together with the minimum of friction or argument and who would in the end make an efficient operational bomber crew.

About this time I had met George Dunn, a sergeant pilot, about the same age as myself. He hailed from Whitstable in Kent and before coming into the RAF had been employed by Pickfords, the removal and travel company. We were both very keen on sport and often played football together. We appeared to have a good rapport going between us so it was decided we should crew together.

Next to join us was Reginald McCadden, a flying officer navigator, who was a Belfast man, about 27 years of age and married. He had been employed in local government and was studying for an economics degree before coming into the Service. Like George and myself he was very keen on sport and all three of us seemed to be on the same wavelength.

Reg introduced us to Flying Officer Joe Scrivener who was to become our mid upper gunner. Joe was a bundle of fun and one seldom found him without a smile on his face. He was from London, married, and was a few years older than Reg. Before the RAF he had been involved in a good retailing business and used to tell us he had many contacts in the City of London and he could always find someone to supply goods that were in short supply. His cheery chatter always kept us amused and he could always be relied on to come up with a funny story when least expected.

Sergeant Jock Todd was about 28 years of age and hailed from Montrose. He was married with a keen sense of humour and was also keen on sport; he was to fit into our crew as the wireless operator. Jock often would say to me, 'Let's not spend too much time in the target area. I am too young to die.'

Sergeant Dixie Dean, a young Canadian from Toronto, was to

be our rear gunner. He was only about 19 years of age and was full of life. His favourite saying when things were not going right for him was, 'You goddam son of a bitch.' A very headstrong young man with his own ideas on how to live life to the full.

Our crew now complete we were all ready to proceed to the next stage of our training, so just to keep us on the move, it was decided that we would move to RAF Lossiemouth's satellite airfield at Elgin.

The airfield at Elgin stood amongst the hills, a few miles from the town. The locals called the locality around the airfield bogs and main and it was truly a beautiful area from a scenic point of view. The only thing that was a little worrying was that these beautiful hills of heather seemed awfully close to the airfield. However I guess we could not have everything and at least we were a very long way from any enemy action.

During the months of January and February 1943, the weather in the Highlands was cold but many of the days and nights were clear with good visibility and gave us good flying weather. The flying exercises we carried out were often difficult and exacting and certainly much more difficult than anything I had experienced in my Canadian training. I suppose one had to remember we were now operating -as a new crew in a real bomber and getting very near to actual operational flying conditions. Our crew seemed to be working well together and the results being achieved seemed to be satisfying our instructors.

Our long cross country trips by day and night and our day and night bombing and gunnery exercises were soon part of our daily routine and with weather conditions holding good we were piling up flying hours and moving through the many exercises that made up our course. We were most fortunate that we had little aircraft unserviceability. I only remember one serious incident when one of our engines packed up when on exercise over the North Sea. We had no trouble making base on one; nevertheless a worrying time.

Other crews on the course seemed to be plagued with trouble and during our training period at Elgin and Lossiemouth, some

Refuelling a training Wellington at 20 OTU, Lossiemouth, 1944

24 aircrew were killed on flying exercises – all very frightening considering we had not seen a shot fired in anger.

On 4th March 1943 the whole crew heaved a sigh of relief and gave a great cheer as we completed our final flying exercise on this operational training course at Elgin.

Although our training at Elgin had been concentrated and demanding we had always found a few spare nights to sample the fine Scottish brew in the local bars and hotels where the friendly landlords made we servicemen so welcome, often into the small hours of the morning.

I would be sorry to leave this fine highland town with its friendly people, its peaceful setting, where the restaurants still had bacon, eggs and chips on their menu. The first week of March saw us pack our kit and say farewell to our highland friends as we headed home for a two week well earned leave.

At the end of my leave I was quite looking forward to reporting to my new station which was RAF Rufforth on the south side of the city of York. I had never been to York before except passing through the rail station on my way from England

37

to Scotland, so I was keen to explore this beautiful city as soon as I got the opportunity. I reported to RAF Rufforth on 24th March 1943 where our crew would convert to Halifax bombers. This was a big improvement to the Wellingtons and four engines were better than two anytime.

On arrival at Rufforth we had an additional member join our crew. He was Ferris Newton, a sergeant flight engineer. A Yorkshireman from Horsborough near Leeds, where he had been landlord owner of the Old Ball Hotel before enlisting. He was married and his wife, Cath, continued running the hotel in his absence. He was a very friendly person in his late twenties who seemed immediately to fit into our now closely knit crew.

On looking over the Halifax for the first time it was magnificent to behold, with four Hercules engines and its completely metal covered airframe; a big improvement on the fabric clad Wellington with only two engines. Inside there was the new Gee radio equipment which enabled a navigator to pinpoint his position with a great degree of accuracy, certainly a great improvement from dead reckoning navigation which depended to a great extent on seeing the ground, or in the case of astro navigation on seeing the stars.

There was the Mark XIV bombsight with its computer unit and sighting head. What a difference this was from the Mark IX sight which was a compass bowl and wire and beads affair and was completely manually operated. The new bombsight was a bomb aimer's dream and provided correct settings were made and it was operated properly, this was a very accurate piece of equipment. I just couldn't wait to try it out.

Many other pieces of up-to-date equipment made this one of the most modern bombers in the world and what a delight it was comparing it to the aircraft we had been accustomed to during our previous training. The whole crew enthused about this mighty bomber and now it would only take us a few weeks to train and familiarize ourselves with the new equipment before moving on to an RAF operational Halifax squadron.

The five weeks we spent converting at Rufforth seemed to go in a flash as we were kept so busy and there seemed so much to take in about our new aircraft. The whole crew enjoyed flying in Halifaxes and the main feature was that George liked flying this large bomber and seemed very much at home with the additional two engines. I felt our time at Rufforth had been well spent and when we finished the course on the 2nd May 1943 it was quite apparent that we were now fully trained and ready to take our places on an operational squadron.

CHAPTER V

76 Squadron, Linton-on-Ouse

The very next day we were posted to 76 Squadron stationed at Linton-on-Ouse in Yorkshire operating Halifax B1 aircraft. Linton was a station in 4 Group Bomber Command and accommodated both 76 and 78 Halifax Squadrons.

By May 1943 the whole of Bomber Command was growing at a tremendous rate as hundreds of Lancasters, Halifaxes and Mosquitoes rolled off the production lines. The Commonwealth Air Training Scheme was paying dividends as thousands of trained aircrew were returning from the USA and Commonwealth countries to join the battle. Commonwealth countries were also making their own contribution as they sent their own young airmen to fight in the bomber offensive.

Morale in the British Isles was high and great credit for this was due to the nightly bombing raids which were striking at the heart of Germany. The United States Army Air Force was also playing a major role daily with their B17 Flying Fortress Missions over Europe. These raids did much to stretch the German ground and air defences to their limits. With the RAF at night and the Americans during the day, the Germans had round the clock bombing to contend with.

During the first five months of 1943 our ground forces were advancing to victory in North Africa, aided by increasing air cover, and the Russians were beginning to hold the enemy on the Eastern Front. Yet it still seemed that the opening of a Second Front was still a long way off and any seaborne attack on Germany's Fortress Europe was still very much in the planning and preparation stages.

Royal Air Force Linton-on-Ouse was a pre-war RAF station with good runways, good hangar accommodation, excellent mess and living accommodation, but with two fully operational squadrons on the station, living accommodation was tight, so it was not surprising that the NCOs in our crew found ourselves quartered at Benningborough Hall, the mansion house residence of Lady Chesterfield at Newton-on-Ouse, a couple of miles from the RAF station. This magnificent house had been taken over by the RAF for the duration of hostilities and it was our good fortune to have the Blue Room on the second floor as our dormitory along with about another ten NCOs, but we were not pushed for space.

The house stood in beautiful grounds on the banks of the River Ouse and oh how wonderful it was to walk by the river and try and forget the horrors of war. During our first couple of weeks at Linton we were being instructed on the final details we would require for our forthcoming sorties. On the flying side we carried out a night cross country and two bull's eye night exercises which were designed as far as possible to simulate a bombing raid. All these flights were about five hours in duration. Added to these we had some formation flying and dropped some practice bombs.

At this point I felt that our aircrew training had been of the highest standard and would go far in assuring the success of our missions and would do much in helping us to keep alive.

The 23rd May 1943 was to be a date I would not easily forget, for about lunch time that day I was to learn from the battle order displayed on the sergeants' mess notice board that Sergeant Dunn and crew were detailed for operations that night. So this was the day we had trained for and our war effort was about to commence. I remember thinking perhaps I should be more excited but I seemed to be looking forward to finding out what it was all about over Europe and to find out for myself just how frightening an experience it would be. In our battledress was placed our escape kit which would be invaluable if shot down in Europe and was endeavouring to escape to one of the neutral countries. The pack was in a perspex box about six inches by

41

four inches and a little over an inch deep. The main contents being a folded rubber water bag, vitamin tablets, a few biscuits and sweets, a few cigarettes, a compass and some water purification tablets.

As the time approached for our pre-operations meal George, myself and the other NCOs in the crew made our way from our quarters at Benningborough to the sergeants' mess on the station where I ate a hearty meal. As we ate our meal we joked and laughed and did our best to play down the tension that perhaps was building up inside. Like me, I am sure the others in the crew felt a great curiosity about the many problems we soon would have to face and just exactly how we would cope under fire. With appetites satisfied we collected our necessary maps and charts and equipment we needed for briefing and headed towards the briefing room.

The briefing room was a long-shaped room which contained 20 or 30 trestle tables surrounded by chairs of the fold-up variety. The side walls had no windows to the outside, or if they did they had been blacked out. These walls were covered in posters on many subjects, but mainly giving warnings about security and the need to be on one's guard at all times when talking about operational matters. At the far end of the room was a low platform with lectern and at the rear of this platform was a very large topographical map of the United Kingdom and the continent of Europe. The map was covered by large patches of coloured perspex denoting the known concentrations of flak and searchlights and from what I could see, there were very few clear areas in Germany. Essen and the Ruhr cities, Berlin and all the other major industrial centres had great concentrations of defensive armament.

The crews were now taking their places around the tables and were chatting and smoking as they awaited the arrival of the squadron commander who would remove the cover from the wall map under which was our target for tonight. Reg and myself busied ourselves spreading out our maps ready to draw in our tracks as soon as the target and route was known.

A few minutes passed and then a great silence fell upon the

room and through the cigarette smoke I could see the squadron commander move the curtain covering the target and this revealed our target to be Dortmund. The stretched pinned tape on the map showed our route via several turning points to the target – then continuing through the aiming point – to more turning points for our return journey to base. Using various turning points enroute and not flying direct to a target did much to confuse the enemy and often he would not know what city was going to be attacked until it actually happened.

The briefing started by the squadron commander giving the target, the route and the type of marking to be used by Pathfinder Force. He was followed by the Met Man who gave us the up-to-date weather enroute and what we could expect in the target area. The weather was good over the North Sea and for most of our route, but a little broken cloud was expected in the target area, but he assured us no difficulty would be experienced in identifying the aiming point. Following the weather man came the navigation leader, bombing leader, signals leader, gunnery leader, engineer leader and last but not least, the intelligence officer.

All these leaders gave their own particular crew members the details they required for the operation to Dortmund. I was particularly interested in what the bombing leader had to say as this was to be my little contribution towards what we hoped would be a successful crew effort. He gave the bomb load which was mixed high explosives and incendiaries, the stations on which the bombs had been positioned in the fuselage, how they had been fused and to what switches they had been wired on the bomb aimer's panel in the nose of the aircraft, settings required for the bombsight computer unit, camera settings for operation with the photo flash carried. He reminded us about manual release mechanism should the electric units fail. I only hoped I would not forget anything I had been told because I did want these bombs to be effective and fall on the correct aiming point.

The intelligence officer gave us all the up-to-date information about Dortmund and suggested aids in helping us to identify our aiming point. He had up-to-date information on the defences in

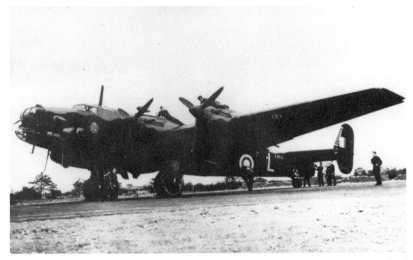

A Halifax B Mk 1, Series II of 76 Squadron. L9530, MP-L, was the personal aircraft of Pilot Officer C. Cheshire (brother of Len, VC). He was shot down over Berlin on the 12/13th August 1941, and taken POW.

Two Halifax bombers on their bombing run pass over the German battle-cruiser *Gneisenau* which has received a direct hit on her starboard side in the pens at Brest, December 1941.

and around Dortmund and heavy concentrations of flak and searchlights to be avoided enroute and Royal Navy ships in the North Sea to be avoided. The RN did not like either friendly or enemy aircraft overflying them during the hours of darkness. His final words of wisdom were should we be so unlucky as to fall into enemy hands we must divulge only our number, rank and name and no other information.

The squadron commander wished us well and the navigation officer asked us to syncronize our watches and our briefing was over.

Reg and I, overlooked by George, busied overselves with the completion of our tracks and timing details on maps and charts. Reg prepared our flight plan using the Met man's forecasted winds. The timing of an operation of this sort was of the utmost importance as we had been given a time for bombing, so it was imperative we arrived on time, as several other waves of bombers were taking part and each wave would have been allocated times to bomb. The Pathfinder Force would be marking the target and our orders were to bomb the coloured target indicators at the times given.

All maps and charts collected from the table, placed in order and put into the green canvas navigation bag along with the other bits and pieces and not forgetting our sextant, it was time to make our way to the flying clothing locker room at the hangars on the edge of the airfield. We all chatted happily as we clad ourselves in our one-piece flying suits and suede flying boots with white stockings turned over their tops. I wore a large white polo necked sweater under my battledress blouse and, with my flying suit on top, hoped I would keep snug and warm. My helmet I carried in my navigation bag as I made my way to collect my parachute and harness along with my Mae West lifejacket. I felt quite ladened down as I walked the short distance to our bus collecting point outside the hangar.

It was about an hour and a quarter before take off as the bus picked us up and we were on our way to our aircraft dispersal point near the far perimeter fence of the airfield. Our timing was good as we were required to be at our aircraft about an hour before take-off and we were pretty well spot on time. All aircraft were kept dispersed round the perimeter of the airfield to minimize damage should an enemy air attack take place.

The bus dropped us at dispersal and there was our aircraft, J for Johnnie, standing in its concrete pen, its outline just visible in the darkness. On moving closer one could see the chocks in position and the starter battery wheeled under the nose ready for connection. There was our ground staff waiting to welcome us and help us with our parachutes and other clothes. They assured us that the aircraft was fully serviceable, fully fuelled, fully bombed, ready for action. Never let us forget these wonderful men of the RAF ground staff without whom, with their technical skills and hard work, no aircraft could ever have got airborne. They knew this was our first operation and they did all in their power to see we were given a very cheery send off with all their best wishes for our safe return.

With about 50 minutes to take-off each one of the crew busied himself with his pre-flight checks and I did likewise. First the position of bombs in the fuselage and their fusing mechanisms. This was all OK and correctly connected. The photo flash when released as our bombs were falling, would give sufficient light for the camera in the nose of the aircraft to record the accuracy of our bombing.

The outside checks complete, it was inside to the bomb aimer's compartment in the nose. Bombsight sighting head and computer unit checked and settings made as required. Camera checked as being correctly positioned and wired. Bomb selection switches noted as correct for bomb stations being used. All bombing equipment was now checked to my satisfaction, so I laid out my route and target maps in order and adjusted the red dimmed compartment light which was the only illumination I had for map reading. I placed my parachute on the starboard side of my compartment and remember thinking I hope I do not need to use that bundle.

With only about thirty minutes to take-off time, I took myself outside to have a smoke and a final chat before taking to the air. All the crew seemed quite chatty, but one could sense a certain amount of underlying tension that everyone was trying to play down. I felt on this first operation as I did on all my later sorties that the period just prior to take-off was always the most tense. Once airborne, there was so much to attend to that one forgot the tensions and concentrated on the job in hand.

About ten minutes before take-off all the crew were on board and George was starting up engines; as I sat in the second pilot's seat he carried out the pre-flight checks. He satisfied himself the aircraft was serviceable and waved the ground crew to remove the chocks from the wheels. Then we waved goodbye as we started to taxi slowly along the dimly lit perimeter track towards the take-off end of the runway in use. Approaching the runway we found three aircraft ahead of us on the track awaiting their signal for take-off, but as aircraft were taking off at fairly close intervals it seemed only a short time before we were lining up with the runway and receiving a green light from the control caravan placed to the starboard of the runway in use.

George started pushing the four throttles forward and as instructed I put my hand behind the throttles to ensure they remained forward. As we gained speed they were pushed fully forward producing full power. As the engines churned the night air we reached flying speed and the aircraft rose gently, perhaps struggling somewhat under the load of bombs, to climb away from the airfield, onwards and upwards towards the stars that hung like signposts in a velvet sky. I sighed as Reg passed the first course to George and we turned on our new heading as we settled down to climb steadily towards our first turning point on the English coast. I scrambled down from the second pilot's seat to my bomb aimer's position in the nose, where I would be in a prone position for the majority of the flight.

The first obstacle of taking off safely had been overcome and we were still climbing upwards to our operational height of 18,000 feet. The English coast should be coming up soon, so I picked up my map and started to map read as I did want to be able to pass Reg a good pinpoint as we crossed the coast outward bound. It was not too long before the coast showed up ahead of us, but as we had no moonlight, only starlight, it was no easy task to pick up our position on the coast. As my eyes became more accustomed to the dark I was able to tell Reg when the coast was crossed and that we were near enough on track. Reg passed the new heading to George to steer, as still climbing, we made our way over the North Sea. It was not too long before we levelled out at our operational height with our nose pointed towards the continent of Europe. We knew there were many bombers in the stream, all heading in the same direction. We did see some, but not as many as I thought we might. The captain kept warning the crew to look out for our own aircraft and for German fighters trying to infiltrate the bomber stream.

The time we spent over the sea was quite uneventful, but as we approached the enemy coast we could see sporadic bursts of light and heavy flak coming up from some of the offshore islands. Things were relatively quiet as we crossed the Dutch coast. I was trying desperately to pinpoint our position. I passed to the navigator what I thought was our position and from his remarks we appeared to be bang on track as a new course was passed to the pilot who headed the aircraft towards a turning point about 60 miles north of Dortmund. This route was designed to steer us through the less dense flak areas, but as I was to find out, there was no easy way through the Ruhr defences. Some routes perhaps were a little less severe than others. Holland produced sporadic bursts of Ack-Ack fire and the odd searchlight waving aimlessly across the sky. From the reports of Joe and Dixie, our gunners, there appeared to be some night fighter flares far off to our port in the North Holland area, but as we ploughed on towards the next turning point we were not to see any fighters, thank goodness.

As we reached our turning point, north of Dortmund and turned on to course for target, we still had about 50 miles to run, but as I looked out ahead I could now see the Pathfinder Force dropping flares and just a little later coloured target indicators were cascading on to the target. Large amounts of light and heavy flak was being thrown up and the sky was ablaze with hundreds of searchlights trying to pick out the bomber stream. The searchlights appeared to be working in cones of about a dozen or so and seemed to cluster round a blue-coloured master radar controlled searchlight. When the master searchlight picked out a bomber its ten or so satellites seemed to cone the poor chap, making him a sitting duck for the Ack-Ack gunners, so a bomber had to look lively if he was to avoid destruction.

With the target indicators apparently placed accurately on the aiming point, the first waves of bombers were now dropping their bombs. Reg passed me a wind for the bombsight and I set it on the computer, at the same time trying to guide George through the flak and searchlights which seemed to be increasing every minute as we neared the city of Dortmund. With a few miles still to run it was time for me to forget guiding us through the defences and concentrate on my bombsight sighting head, trying to guide our aircraft on to a course that would bring the target indicators down the reflector plate to the release point.

As I looked down through my reflector plate on the final part of our bombing run there was a panorama set out below me that must have been the world's greatest firework display. There were the red target indicators on the ground and greens cascading above the aiming point. There were the high explosive bombs bursting on the ground; there were the incendiary bombs causing fires throughout the city; there was the light flak coming up to about 8,000 feet; there were the bursts of red tracer bullets as they streamed across the sky. Worst of all were the black bursts of the heavy anti-aircraft shells just below and on either side of our aircraft. The searchlights were making it look like daylight outside and this showed many other bombers very near and I only hoped we would not collide.

There was little we could do now to avoid flak and searchlights as we were committed to our bombing run and with bomb doors open, I was passing the:

'Left, Left'

'Right'

'Steady'

signals to George who was doing a magnificent job in edging the

49

aircraft on to a track bringing the aiming point down the centre line of my bombsight.

'Hold it steady there, George', and in a few more seconds the target had reached the bomb release point on my sighting head. A good hard push on the bomb release button in my right hand and the bombs were falling from the bomb bay. Having watched them all go I called for: 'Bomb doors closed,' as I tried to follow the bombs down and watched our photo flash explode and hoped we had got a good photograph.

As we moved through the target area and across the city I was convinced that it was well nigh impossible to traverse this holocaust without being hit. However we were turning and weaving and George was doing an excellent job, as I tried to guide him through the miles of concentrated flak. Reg passed our new course to steer and George quickly turned the aircraft westward towards Holland and the North Sea. We appeared to be clearing the Ruhr defences very slowly and it would be about fifteen minutes or so before the pressure on us seemed to subside. The sky ahead seemed to have been laid with German night fighter flares to aid their fighters in infiltrating the bomber stream. George warned the crew to be particularly alert as we were passing near the flare lit part of the sky.

As we sped towards the enemy coast we were now only experiencing small amounts of heavy flak in sporadic bursts, but still had a feeling that night fighters were very active, but we seemed to be running the gauntlet. It was a great relief to me as we approached the enemy coast and through the small amount of broken cloud I tried to pinpoint our position as we crossed to be over the comparative safety of the North Sea. The new course was set and it was 'Home George, and don't spare the revs.' The North Sea was quite peaceful except for the odd burst of flak far away to our port and I could only guess that perhaps some of our aircraft had strayed too near to some Royal Navy ship down in the Channel area.

The first indication we had that we were nearing the English coast was when a few searchlights from the coastal defences seemed to be waving us home as they swept across the night sky.

A 76 Squadron Halifax MP-D is air-tested by Pilot Officer Len Smith in August 1941.

The Office — the pilot's cockpit in a Halifax.

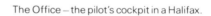

What a beautiful sight and how wonderful to know that in a few minutes we would be back to the safety of England. The coast was crossed and we altered course for base and soon we were picking up airfield identification letters, usually two letters being flashed out on a beacon near the airfield. We were now pinpointing our position easily and accurately. From my reading of the identification letters I knew we would soon be crossing the Humber and it would not be long before we would pick up the Linton identification letters.

Sure enough, there they were ahead, so George called the air traffic and requested instructions for landing. The air traffic controller acknowledged our call and gave us number twelve position for landing. This meant we would be flying around for some considerable time before getting back on the ground. By this time I had taken up my position in the second pilot's seat, pleased to get up from my prone position in the bomb aimer's compartment. I was feeling more relaxed as I could see our airfield below, but still vigilance had to be maintained as we looked into the night sky because often enemy aircraft had been known to penetrate airfield defences and shoot down incoming bombers or make a mess of the runways where they were landing.

I remember thinking what horrible luck it would be to be shot down over one's own base after having survived for hours over enemy territory.

By this time I was desperate for a cigarette and wished we could land a lot sooner, but we just had to bide our time and it was not too long before we were making our final approach to the runway in use. The wheels were going down and the lights on the ground were funnelling in towards the runway and it was only a short time before we could see the runway ahead and it was over a few more hedges and our wheels were screeching on to the end of the runway as we smoothly touched down and rolled to our turn-off point near the far end of the runway. It was a great feeling to be back on terra firma having completed our first operational sortie.

We taxied to our dispersal point and there was much joyful

chatter between the crew as we prepared to disembark. Steps were lowered at the rear door and we clambered out on to the tarmac. What a great feeling to be alive and oh how very good that cigarette tasted as we chatted to our ground staff and climbed on to the crew bus which would take us round the perimeter track to the hangars where we could return our safety equipment and then it would be on to debriefing.

Debriefing was always a happy place for those who had survived and were there to give their views and reports on how their part of the operation had been carried out. On arrival a cup of coffee was thrust into one's hand and this laced with a tot of rum made it taste very good. This wonderful feeling was still upon me as I felt so relieved to know we had survived the flak, the searchlights, the night fighters and were there to fight another day. At least next time I would know what to expect and I only hoped that all our operations would be as trouble free as this sortie to Dortmund.

The debriefing was quite exacting and so it should be. Questions like:

'What was the aiming point looking like to you?'

'Did you bomb the correct target indicators dropped by the Pathfinders?'

'What general detail, if any, could you identify?'

'Did the bombs appear to be straddling the aiming point and were they concentrated?'

'How much light or heavy flak did you encounter and how accurate?'

'Did you encounter much night fighter activity and what fighter flares if any had been laid?'

'Did you see any of our bombers in difficulty or being shot down and if so did you see any parachutes coming from the damaged bombers?'

'Did your photo flash operate and did the camera take a photograph?'

From all these questions posed to each crew, answers would be given so that the pieces of the jigsaw would all fit together to give an overall picture of the raid and its success or otherwise and these results would be confirmed when the aerial photographs had been developed.

Just as we finished debriefing we were to find that two of our squadron aircraft had failed to return. One could only hope that the fourteen crew members had escaped death, even if it meant spending some time in a prisoner of war camp.

Making our way back to our sleeping quarters at Benningborough Hall I stopped at the telephone box in the village of Linton to call my parents and let them know I was safe as the early morning radio news would be giving the target attacked and also the number of aircraft that had failed to return and this could be quite worrying for parents. It must have been about 7 a.m. when I turned into my bed in the Blue Room dormitory at Benningborough Hall. It had been a long night and being very tired, I fell into a deep sleep.

It was about midday on 24th May when we had struggled out of bed, washed and shaved and made our way to the sergeants' mess for lunch and to find if our name appeared on any operational orders for that night. We were to find that no operation was planned and our crew was therefore free till next morning. It was a nice sunny day and after lunch, myself and some others in the crew paid a visit to a little teashop in Linton Village where some very kind ladies served up an excellent cup of tea in their front garden. This teashop being so near the RAF station was very popular with aircrew and off duty WAAFS and it was so relaxing sitting around in the sun and comparing experiences with more experienced crews. It was times like this when one realised the camaraderie that existed amongst aircrew, not forgetting the WAAF. God bless them for doing so much to ensure the operational efficiency of bomber stations.

After our evening meal we were off exploring the grounds of Benningborough Hall making our way over the lush green meadows in front of the house and down to where the River Ouse flowed through the estate. It was a still quiet evening and how wonderful to be alive and to gaze on this beautiful part of Yorkshire.

Along the river bank we came upon a gentleman known by the

name of Nick who owned a rowing boat and was doing a roaring trade ferrying RAF boys across the river so that they could visit the Alice Hawthorn pub in the beautiful village of Nun Monkton, so we paid our few pennies and were soon climbing up the opposite bank on our way to explore this new drinking place.

What a beautiful village this turned out to be. In front of the pub was a village green with a maypole and a duck pond at one end. I was intrigued with the various types of houses that surrounded the green as many of them seemed pretty old, although some were of brick construction, they all seemed in a pretty good state of repair and had been well looked after. The whole scene looking from the pub window was one of peace and tranquillity and a far cry from what we had experienced over the Ruhr Valley on the previous night. The Alice Hawthorn proved to be a friendly pub serving a decent pint of beer and where happy chatter and a bit of community singing seemed to be the order of the day.

Next day, the 25th, saw the crew down at the mess for an early breakfast then over to the crew room to await the battle order of the day. It was just before lunch we knew that we were again on the battle order for that night. We noted the times for meals and briefing and it was then back to Benningborough to relax for a few hours before preparing for our second sortie. The weather was holding good and as it was a period of no moon in the early hours of the morning, conditions were ideal for the heavy bomber offensive.

I remember lying on top of my bed that afternoon thinking how well our first operation had gone and only hoped and prayed that perhaps we might be lucky and survive our tour of 30 operational sorties. I was feeling a little more confident now that I knew what to expect over Germany, but it was always at the back of my mind that only about 10% of aircrew were completing a tour of 30 operations. I suppose everyone thought somehow or other they could survive and I consoled myself with the fact that our crew were knitting together like a good team and so together I hoped we could beat the odds.

All the crew seemed quite cheery as we all met in the briefing room to find our target was Düsseldorf. Well, there it was, back again to the Ruhr or Happy Valley as it was known by aircrew. We could expect a similar flak and searchlight reception to that which had greeted us at Dortmund as there was no hiding place in the Ruhr skies.

Our flight enroute to Düsseldorf was quite uneventful, but the flak barrage in and around the target area was quite intense. It was amazing how a little cloud in the sky made one feel a little less exposed to the ground defences. We weaved our way through the Ack-Ack shells bursting all around us and were able to make a good bombing run through the actual target area and I was able to see quite clearly the green target indicators dropped by the Pathfinder Force which were showing up as huge green blobs on the built-up area of the city and I had no difficulty in identifying them amongst the many fires what were burning through the city.

As the aiming point was reached on the bombsight and we dispatched our bomb load and closed the bomb doors it was back to weaving our way through the shells and the searchlights, but it was not too long before the barrage slackened a bit and I felt we were through the worst. There were still lots of searchlights very active and our skipper was telling all to:

'Keep a good lookout for night fighters.'

There seemed to be fighter flares being dropped some distance off to our starboard and from the tracer bullets screaming across the sky there was obviously a great amount of activity by the German night fighters. I was feeling quite pleased we had cleared the Ruhr defences and were running clear of the demon fighter aircraft so I breathed a sigh of relief as we crossed the enemy coast and was pleased to have the North Sea below us and had no shells bursting around us. We were homeward bound with no damage and the four engines churning their way through the night sky as we sped towards the English coast to arrive at Linton at 05.00 in nice time for an early breakfast. The sortie to Düsseldorf had only taken us five hours and fifteen minutes for the round trip so it was quite a fast sortie and from our crew point of view, a very successful one.

A 76 Squadron Halifax Mk I in flight.

The 27th May saw us on our way to the industrial heartland of the Ruhr to the city of Essen, home of the Krupps armament works, steel foundries, factories and workshops, all producing weapons of war to fuel the German war machine.

We had left the North Sea behind us and were about 40 or 50 miles from the Ruhr and as I looked ahead from the bomb aimer's position in the nose of the aircraft, what I saw, to say the least of it, was a bit frightening. As we approached Essen from the south the whole of the Ruhr seemed to have erupted with hundreds of searchlights sweeping across the sky making it look like daylight up at 17,000 feet. Thousands of Ack-Ack shells were bursting all round the sky and tracer bullets were whizzing across ahead of us at about our flight level. I had never felt quite so exposed as I looked at the barrage that was facing us. There appeared to be no way through as the flak barrage increased and there were many areas with concentrated squares of flak which was known as Box Barrage and were filling the sky with complete walls of shells. To me the odds of getting into Essen and out again without being hit were not at all good.

Lying on my stomach with my head over the bombsight sighting head, I did my best to give the captain instructions to try to guide us through this deadly barrier, but it was heavy and bursting all around us and I wondered how long before a shell would hit us, as I could hear a noise from time to time like someone beating a dustbin and I knew they were getting near and I am sure my heart missed a beat. It was time for me to concentrate on my bombsight and try to guide George on to the target indicators and this concentration seemed to make one's fears disappear. All my thoughts were now to get our bombs down on the target indicators. As I guided our skipper on to a course that brought the target markers down the centre line of my bombsight reflector plate towards the release point. We seemed to be such a long time straight and level for these few minutes just before I pressed the bomb release button and watched the bombs leave the aircraft and make their way down between the bursting Ack-Ack shells.

As I called for, 'Bomb Doors Closed,' and the skipper

complied with my request I had a quick look at the whole target area which had a large number of fires burning all over the city and there were the high explosive bombs exploding in the built-up area, but my main thought was to get the hell out of this flak-laden sky as I had seen several of our aircraft being shot down and I did not want to meet the same fate, but it seemed some little time before we appeared to be clear of the Ruhr Defences and over the Low Countries on our way to the North Sea. I remember thinking as we crossed the enemy coast and were over the North Sea, I hope we do not have to visit Essen too often because although we had managed to survive without being hit, I would not gamble that luck of this sort could continue. It seemed to me a miracle that we had not been hit on this occasion. I felt we had probably seen, next to Berlin, the most heavily defended city in Germany. The whole crew had been magnificent and under the most devastating flak barrage had managed to force home the attack.

We were pleased to get back to Linton and step out on to that airfield and feel the cool morning air hitting our faces and making us feel so wonderful to be still alive.

Harris again ordered the squadron back to the Ruhr on 29th May, the target being Wuppertal Barman. The target was not one of the bigger Ruhr cities, but quite industrial and playing its part in fuelling the German war machine and important enough for Harris to send his bomber force.

The weather conditions over Wuppertal were ideal for bombing, a clear night sky with good visibility. When over the target area I was able to pick out quite a lot of ground detail and the Pathfinders had done a great job dropping their target indicators right on aiming point. Our run up to bomb release was certainly not as hazardous as we had experienced at Essen, but nevertheless there was a fair number of shells reaching up into the bomber stream and near enough to treat them with great respect. Looking down on Wuppertal I was able to see huge fires burning throughout the built-up area and high explosive bombs were bursting around the red and green target indicators burning brightly around our aiming point.

After a trouble-free bombing run on to the target and placing our bombs as accurately as possible, it was a little more weaving to escape the searchlights and Reg was passing George our course for our exit point on the enemy coast. Joe and Dixie, our gunners, were not reporting much fighter activity so it was an uneventful trip home.

The squadron despatched twelve bombers on this operation and all carried out successful sorties and all returned to base safely, so from the squadron point of view, a good bombing attack with no casualties. I only wished they could all be like that.

By May 1943 the Battle of the Ruhr was well and truly being pursued by 'Butch' Harris and his staff as on many occasions forces of 500 bombers or more were being dispatched on the heavier raids on the industrial heartland of the Reich and it looked as if the enemy's industries were taking a pounding as more and more towns and cities felt the weight of bombs from many hundreds of bombers.

A battle of this sort is not fought without casualties and aircrew casualties were considerable, many more than one cared to dwell upon. However, I consoled myself with the thought that the destruction and casualties being inflicted on the enemy far outweighed anything they could inflict on the bomber force.

The destruction being wrought upon German foundries, factories, workshops and all work places producing for or working for the German war effort was enormous. The persistent interruption of the work schedules and the disorganization of workers' homes and communications must have been greatly curtailing the factory output and interfering with the morale in some way or other of all the labour force.

Added to RAF bomber command sorties were the daylight sorties being carried out by the United States Army Air Force; their Flying Fortresses (B17s) were keeping the German defences stretched to their limits for most hours of the day and night. The German fighter aircraft were having limited success against the bombers, but were not without their own casualties especially against the fighter aircraft accompanying the USAAF bombers and from the Flying Fortresses themselves. The USAAF aircrew in Flying Fortresses fought courageously in the skies over Europe and were often under attack for hours at a time from the German fighter aircraft.

The beginning of June 1943 was anything but flaming, in fact it was more like monsoon rain that hit us, explained by the Meteorological Office as a series of fronts affecting both the UK and the Continent. The conditions were to keep us grounded from operational flying till 11th June. During our crew's enforced grounding, George and myself did not waste our time but managed to carry out a night vision course at RAF Driffield which lasted a few days and proved quite interesting especially the simulated bombing exercises carried out on the bombing teacher which was quite a sophisticated machine being very good for map reading and target identification training.

Much to my surprise both George and myself were deemed to have exceptional night vision. This was very comforting to know. At least we would be able to see our enemy as quickly as he was likely to see us in varying degrees of darkness.

On 11th June it was back to our war effort as we were ordered to Düsseldorf. I did not mind this target too much as having been there before we knew what to expect, I just wished we could get a break from the Ruhr targets. However I did not think there was much hope of this as the Ruhr seemed to be Harris's first priority.

On the way to and from the target area we encountered quite a bit of cloud, but over the city the cloud was broken and the target markers were visible through the spaces in the clouds and the main force bombers seemed to have started many fires as both incendiaries and high explosive bombs were falling around the markers in the built-up area of the city.

After clearing the defences of the target area from my observations below the aircraft and from remarks by Joe and Dixie, our gunners, it was obvious that German night fighters were amongst the bomber stream and from the many tracer bullets streaming across the night sky they appeared to be there in strength. George kept warning the crew to keep their eyes skinned for fighters and it was only a little later that a Ju 88 passed about 1,000 feet below us going like hell in the opposite direction, so we just hoped he would keep going. On this sortie I felt there was much more German fighter activity than we had experienced previously and they certainly seemed to lay many more fighter flares to illuminate the bomber stream.

We managed to run the gauntlet without being attacked and it was a marvellous feeling of relative safety as we sped across the North Sea leaving the islands of Texel and Terschelling to our rear, firing at any bombers that happened to have strayed within their range of fire. It was always a great feeling after crossing the North Sea when an English searchlight could be picked up as we approached the coast, safety only seemed a short distance away and at least for that night another battle was complete. On arriving at base with aircraft intact and crew safe and sound, I felt elated that our luck was holding and only hoped and prayed that our good fortune would continue.

At debriefing we were to find of the 18 crews the squadron had dispatched, only 16 had returned. I felt sure that the two missing had fallen foul of the fighters, although I had not actually seen any aircraft being shot down. This was when the reality of war struck home and one wondered were the missing crew members lying dead or wounded in a foreign land, trying to escape, or taken prisoner of war. These were the permutations and all I hoped was that they were alive.

There was no respite for 76 Squadron and next night the 12th June saw us continue the Battle of the Ruhr. This time it was Bochum, certainly one of the smaller industrial towns in the Ruhr, but with its steel plant and workshops it was important enough to warrant the attention of Sir Arthur Harris and his bomber force.

From our crew's point of view it was a very good sortie with no trouble enroute or in the target area, but as on the previous night fighter flares laid by the Germans to light the night sky showed that their fighters were very active. Our crew kept very alert and we were lucky enough to escape the agony of having a German fighter pump shells into our aircraft. We returned to

Linton after a 5 hour 40 minute sortie and I wished they could all be as easy as that one to Bochum. The squadron had dispatched fifteen aircraft on the operation of which one had failed to return, so some unfortunate crew had not found the going easy.

Doing a quick calculation I found we had lost six aircraft altogether on the six sorties in which we had been involved, so we were averaging a loss of one per raid. That meant during a tour of 30 operations it was possible the squadron was going to lose 30 aircraft, which to me was rather frightening, as we had 22 operational sorties still to complete. I thought to myself that I had better put that calculation to the back of my mind and hope the rate of loss would decrease.

CHAPTER VI

Holme on Spalding Moor

The operation to Bochum was to be our last sortie from Linton-on-Ouse as the squadron moved to Holme on Spalding Moor on 16th June 1943. Holme was a wartime-built airfield in the Humberside area of Yorkshire. It lay just north of the River Humber and about equidistant between Selby and Beverley and about 18 miles south-west of the city of York.

The reason the squadron moved from Linton was to make room for a Canadian squadron which was one of the squadrons of Six Group, a new group of bomber squadrons being positioned around the Linton-on-Ouse area. The personnel on 76 Squadron were not too enamoured at having to give up our well-built pre-war RAF station at Linton and our beautiful living accommodation at Benningborough Hall. We would miss the beautiful countryside along the valley of the Ouse and the surrounding area where the many small pubs and inns provided such good entertainment and good company for tired airmen, but alas this would now only be a memory.

It was the afternoon of 16th June when we landed our Halifax for the first time at Holme on Spalding Moor and were directed to a dispersal point near the perimeter fence of the airfield. As George taxied the aircraft round the perimeter track to our dispersal we all had a good look at our new airfield. The first snag we discovered at our dispersal point was that a tree from an adjoining field came very near to damaging our wing tip, so that the first job for Ferris, our engineer, was to get a saw and see the tree was demolished. If the Germans could not damage our aircraft we were cetainly not going to allow a tree to do so.

After we off-loaded our kit from the Halifax the crew bus came to pick us up and take us to our respective messes where we were allocated our living quarters. The sergeants' and officers' messes at Holme were of wooden prefabricated construction and were within the confines of the base. The NCOs' sleeping quarters in which I was interested were outside the station, a short distance from the main gate. The reason for dispersing quarters in this way was in case of air attack, so that all personnel would not be in the same area. Our sleeping quarters were nissen huts with outside separate wash places and WCs being common to several huts. A big difference from our plush Blue Room dormitory at Benningborough Hall. There were eight NCOs per nissen hut so we were not too badly off for space and the sun was shining outside so we had a lot to be thankful for when one considered the conditions our soldiers and airmen were subjected to in the deserts of North Africa where under canvas it was stinking hot during the day and freezing cold at night and sand got everywhere expecially when a sandstorm blew up. We were fortunate in that providing we could survive our battles over Europe we had a reasonably comfortable bed to come back to and fairly peaceful conditions in which to live and sleep, so I had no moans.

From 16th to 20th June we were not on the battle orders and this allowed us to carry out a couple of air tests lasting about an hour each and gave us plenty of spare time to look over our new station and become familiar with the locations of the various sections. In the evenings we were able to borrow a few bicycles and do a quick reconnaissance of the countryside around the station, locating the local pubs and sampling their particular brand of ale.

The area appeared so bleak after Linton but we had been spoiled there with its lovely scenery and pretty little inns and pubs. There were few pubs in the immediate vacinity of the station and the ones we explored did not seem to appeal to the crew who were really not big drinkers, but enjoyed a walk or cycle run in the evenings to escape from mess and barrack room. Jock, our wireless operator, took a liking to one of the pubs in the village of Holme and I believe became quite a regular visitor. The other crew members I think agreed that social life in their respective messes would be our main entertainment in the evenings. There was always a card game going on and the Canadians on the squadron would have a dice game going and often this was taking place on the floor of the sergeants' mess.

We were fortunate in having a regular bus service from Holme to the city of York and I took advantage of this on many occasions when I had a few off duty hours. York was one of my favourite cities. The Minster, the city walls and all its Roman and other historical places of interest never failed to appeal to my historical interests as did all the older cities in Britain. The city had also an abundance of small hotels, pubs, inns, and hostelries, some being very old and of historical interest, so this all appealed to me and helped to get my mind away from the horror of the skies over the Ruhr.

Betty's Bar in the centre of the city was a fairly large modern pub and restaurant and became the favourite drinking place of the aircrew from the 4 Group and other RAF stations in the vicinity of the city of York. Any night of the week the place was crowded mainly with NCO and officer aircrew, all knocking back the beer and trying to forget what might lie ahead of them on their next operational sortie and who could blame them. I always enjoyed my visits to Betty's Bar and perhaps on occasions drank more than was good for me but I never regretted having done so. Some of our crew including myself would attend the dances which were held in the De Gray Rooms, only a short distance from Betty's and on many occasions several of us who after the dance had missed the last bus for Holme would club together and take a taxi. It never ceased to amaze me how many bodies could pile into a cab but the taxi men were always good-natured and never complained, provided no one was being crushed to death under a heap of bodies.

Our visits to York always gave us the chance to meet friends from other squadrons and compare notes as to how their squadrons were faring in the battle. So often we were to find that someone we had known was reported missing and it was always a blow, but was something that had to be pushed to the back of one's mind with the hope that he was a prisoner of war. On 21st June 1943, we were informed that we were about to carry out our seventh Operational Sortie and guess what? It was back to the Ruhr to Krefeld. We had no difficulty on this operation as everything seemed to go as planned and with good weather the red and green target indicators were easily visible bang on the target area which was near the centre of the town. Large areas of the town seemed to be alight with incendiary bombs as high explosive bombs could be seen exploding on the built-up area. This was a very successful attack and thousands of acres of Krefeld were devastated by the raid so I hoped we did not have to pay another visit as the flak as usual was most deadly, but perhaps not just as concentrated as some of the other Ruhr cities.

All the Holme aircraft had returned safely so we had little to complain about from a squadron point of view.

For the next week Harris was to keep us very busy with raids on 22nd June to Mulheim, 24th to Wuppertal, 25th to Gelsenkirchen and on the 28th to Cologne. The Cologne raid was carried out by bombing through cloud which was completely obscuring the city but it did not stop the German gunners from mounting a very heavy and accurate flak barrage. I felt a bit cheated in not being able to see the city; however one felt a little safer when cloud was obscuring the view of the gunners on the ground, though it did not really make a great deal of difference as their radar predicted anti-aircraft shells were often too accurate for comfort and the only way to fox their radar was to keep weaving when possible.

On leaving Cologne and heading for home the cloud was a bit broken and searchlights kept sweeping across the sky often in large cones of a dozen or more. Just as I thought the flak barrage was abating and we were clearing the target area I was trying to guide George clear of the flak when a master blue searchlight picked us up, illuminating the whole aircraft and I felt we were the only aircraft in the sky. Like a flash there was about six more searchlights on us but George reacted quickly with nose down and weaving frantically.

67

I asked George to weave in the opposite direction of the cone's movement, as this was our method of crossing the cone and being out before the operators on the searchlights could switch direction. We were lucky it seemed to work. We were through and seemed to be moving away from the searchlights, but not before the Ack-Ack shells were bursting all around us but only one got near enough to do any damage, as with one hell of a bang it exploded below the centre fuselage.

My heart missed a beat but our flight engineer soon checked the damage and reported a few small holes but nothing desperate, so we all sighed with relief. I had been convinced that the noise created by that shell exploding just below the aircraft had torn the fuselage apart so was pleased to hear the engineer's report. I thought that the quick action taken by our skipper had allowed us to escape from very accurately controlled searchlights and flak working together. This brought home to me, and I suppose the others in the crew, how quickly situations could arise over enemy territory and how vigilance was so important to our survival.

The remainder of our journey home was quite uneventful and George was calling for landing instructions just before 04.00 hours as we cruised over the Humber towards Holme on Spalding Moor.

*

This was the first time our aircraft had been hit and the nearest we had come to being shot from the sky so one can well imagine the look of relief on our faces as we climbed down the aircraft steps on to terra firma. When we got to debriefing, never was coffee to taste so good as we sat down at the table to relate our story of the raid.

By the time we left the debriefing room we were to know that two of the squadron aircraft had failed to return. We had been lucky, I walked slowly back to my quarters, said a little prayer, turned in and was asleep in a few minutes.

The day after our escape from the defences of Cologne it brought home to me just how fortunate we were to have such a well disciplined efficient crew and at this stage of our tour when squadron losses were high, it was very comforting to know we had the know-how and the ability to survive, providing our luck held. Each morning after we had been on operations, George, Reg and myself would pay a visit to the intelligence section where we would examine our aerial photograph from the previous night and try and assess exactly where our bombs had fallen.

We were also able to get the up to date information on previous raids and the estimated success achieved. I often felt that perhaps a greater amount of information regarding the results of raids could have been made available to aircrew as many of us took a great interest in the overall achievements of the Command. It may have been that the aerial reconnaissance of bombed targets did not show up as much information as we would have liked. I often wondered at Group and Command Headquarters how they managed to put together all the information they had about a raid and how they worked out their assessment. I would suppose on occasions that air reconnaissance photographs would be difficult to read and assess and certainly could not show anything like the detail that pictures at ground level would record. Although only a sergeant it was nice to know that a particular raid on which our crew had been involved was a success and that our efforts were being appreciated. I was and still am one who believes in always keeping troops completely up to date on the state of the battle.

In spare moments I would think just how important was the part that an aircrew member was playing in the overall scheme of things. Would our bombing efforts mean when the time came for our armies to launch their attack on Fortress Europe that their casualties would be fewer? I sincerely hoped that this would be so. If the losses that Bomber Command were encountering were to save thousands of soldiers' lives on the battlefields of Europe when the Second Front started, then we would have played a major part in the overall plan. Added to this, if bombing could shorten the war by any appreciable amount, then our efforts would not be in vain. Thirdly, I hoped that our continuous bombing of Germany would bring the horrors of war home to the German people and ensure they would never embark on such a course ever again; then we would have succeeded.

I often felt that some aircrew did not take very much interest in the overall strategy of the war as they were very much preoccupied, and so they should be, in endeavouring to survive a tour of 30 operational sorties and this was a gigantic war effort to come from any one man considering the survival rate was only around the 10% mark. Every aircrew member was a volunteer and like myself, felt sure that they would not have changed their lot for any less hazardous combat duty.

Guess what? Our next operational sortie was a return to Cologne on 3rd July. The only difference was that our aiming point was in the east of the city and our route was different, so hoped we could dodge the defences. We took off at 23.10 on the 3rd and landed at 04.30 on the 4th. To us the raid proved quite successful as the weather was clear and we could see the high explosive bombs bursting amongst the industrial buildings in the target area. The defences were every bit as fierce as previously, but we managed to get through without damage to aircrew or aircraft. It looked as if Harris was determined to destroy the industrial potential of Cologne including any new buildings or plant that had appeared since the raids of 1942 when in May of that year Bomber Command carried out a 1000 Bomber Raid on the city. I often wondered just how good or how quick the Germans were at rebuilding damaged plant, factories and workshops and felt quite sure they would do a lot in their very thorough, hardworking and efficient way to keep their industries working.

In the early part of July 1943, I could sense an anxiousness amongst several aircrew on the squadron and during our many chats in the sergeants' mess it became apparent that quite a number did not expect to survive a tour of 30 operations. I could understand their thoughts although I myself was never to think along these lines. I think I was more like the old soldier who always thought it would be someone else who would die and not

Pilot Officer George Dunn and crew beside their Halifax of 76 Squadron. Holme-on-Spalding Moor, August 1943. *(Left to right)* Reg McCadden, 'Dixie' Dean, Jock Todd, George Dunn, Ferris Newton, the author, Joe Scrivenor.

To Hamburg, August 1943. The 76 Squadron airman making the 'V' sign to the left of the pigeon box is Sergeant Mauser. The airman on the left in flying boots is Flight Lieutenant Turner.

him. Although my thoughts were always of survival like all other aircrew, I knew we were losing on an average about one or two crews (14 men) missing on each operation. Many of the aircrew would survive and become prisoners of war; however far too many were to die in the skies over Europe.

Even although every aircrew member knew his chances of survival were slim the great majority continued in their endeavour to complete a tour of operations. Only a few fell by the wayside and became known as LMF (Lacking in Moral Fibre). The few LMF cases asked to be removed from operational flying for many diverse reasons, but in the main the reason was the inability to face up to the enemy and his defences. I could feel sorry for many of these men as some tried awfully hard to overcome their nervousness and fear but did not seem to have the strength to surmount the anxiety barrier. Those deemed to be lacking in Moral Fibre were sent to a depot at Chessington where they were stripped of their Flying Brevet, lost their ranks and were posted to ground duties. My opinion about people who became LMF cases was that many had slipped through the aircrew selection procedure and should never have been on aircrew duties in the first place as they lacked the stomach for such a demanding job. Perhaps some did not appreciate just how hazardous bomber operations would be when they volunteered for aircrew duties, so perhaps we should not blame them for trying to make the grade.

I was extremely fortunate in being in a crew where I never knew morale to be anything but high and where we all seemed to knit together to ensure that the cheery patter kept us all in good spirits and this I might say, was a great boon under such trying conditions.

In my own mind the big morale booster was always to keep one's mind active on subjects other than operational flying. Our crew were nearly all interested in sport and football and snooker took up some of our time while our Canadian rear gunner, Dixie, was interested in dice as most Canadians were. Golf was never far from my mind and although my scope was limited I made the best of it. As a crew we always seemed to be going somewhere

and it was always a great break away from the station when
Ferris Newton, our flight engineer, piled us into his Morris 8 car
and transported us to his pub, the Old Ball at Horsborough near
Leeds, where Cath his wife always made us so very welcome and
the regulars in the bar treated us like long lost friends and made
a great fuss of the whole crew. After a couple of days at Leeds
away from Holme and from the war one always returned very
much refreshed and once again ready for the fray.

A trip to the hostelries in York and perhaps followed by a
dance at the De Gray Rooms, a sing song and a few jugs of beer
in the mess, a station dance or an ENSA show were all great
morale boosters and kept one's mind off the horrors of war.

The raid to Gelsenkirken on 9th July was a Wanganui attack
which meant that owing to cloud cover over the target, the
Pathfinder sky markers were dropped by radar in such a position
above the cloud that the main stream bombers could aim their
bombs at these markers and provided they had not drifted too
far from their original position the bombs had a good chance of
hitting somewhere near the intended aiming point below the
cloud. On this occasion it was a good thing that this type of
marking was being used as the tremendous amount of cloud
cover was completely obscuring the target from our height of
18,000 feet.

I never did believe too much in this type of sky-marking as it
was very difficult for the Pathfinder Force who did their best
under the circumstances to mark accurately. Often markers
dropped in the correct position above the clouds would tend to
drift quickly in varying winds and of course the more they drifted
the less accurate would be the bombs dropped through them.
However the chances were they would still fall on the built-up
area of the town or city below the cloud. In circumstances where
cloud cover was so dense and where the bombers would be
endangered by flying at low level below the cloud, this type of
marking at least gave some degree of accuracy.

The extensive cloud cover seemed to extend over a large part
of the Ruhr and although obscuring the many searchlights in the
area it did not prevent the predicted flak from exploding in and

around the bomber stream. We seemed to escape quite rapidly from the flak barrage. With our gunners not reporting any fighter activity around us, we had a peaceful journey back to base and at about 05.00 hours were touching down at Holme on Spalding Moor.

The raid on Gelsenkirken was the crew's thirteenth in succession to the Ruhr and although we knew that the Battle of the Ruhr was probably the greatest battle Bomber Command had ever fought we wondered where and when we might be sent to escape the flak and night fighters of Happy Valley. On 13th July we were on the fourteenth raid of our tour to Aachen on the western edge of the Ruhr and near the Dutch border. The sortie would only take about five hours. It was great how a short trip like this and not having to plough into the middle of the Ruhr seemed to cheer the crew up at this stage of our tour. Any small things that seemed to make our lot less hazardous were very welcome.

The aiming point on this occasion was the main industrial part of the town containing the Phillips works, engineering, armament factories and workshops. There were quite a lot of cloud in the target area but I could see the target indicators through the breaks and was also able to pick up quite a large rail junction or marshalling yard as our bombs sped towards the aiming point. The raid seemed to be going well as there appeared to be fires in the built up area as the high explosive bombs crashed amongst the buildings. The defences were formidable, but not of the ferocity of the larger cities in the area. Their flak bursts were sporadic and haphazard, giving the impression that there was little, if any, predicted flak. As we left the target area it was a relatively short trip over Holland and across the North Sea to the English coast. On the whole we had a quiet sortie and on talking to the other crews involved at debriefing they seemed to have encountered similar conditions.

On our return to base we were to find that there had been some excitement in our absence. It appeared at the take-off stage of the operation that thirteen crews had got airborne safely, but the fourteenth aircraft developed some shimmying on take-off resulting in the undercarriage collapsing and the aircraft skidding off the runway on to the grass where a fire started and the crew dashed at high speed for safety. The crash crew attempted to put out the blaze, but were unable to control the fire and were forced to withdraw. Shortly afterwards with one hell of a bang the whole aircraft blew up and with an even bigger bang the bombs went off, breaking windows in the near vicinity of the airfield and scattering debris over a wide area.

The unfortunate incident meant that only 13 of the 24 aircraft scheduled for the raid were able to take part, but the main factor was there were no casualties in what could have been a very nasty accident. I did not hear any of the aircrew who missed out on the raid complaining. This sort of thing made one think how simple it was to have accidents even in one's own backyard.

*

By the last week of July 1943, Harris and his staff had decided to pay attention to the larger industrial cities out-with the Ruhr so the Battle of Hamburg was to commence on 24th July with the dispatch of over 700 heavy bombers to this large German seaport and important industrial city. The night raid of the 24th was followed by two daylight attacks on the city by the American Eighth Air Force on 25th July.

I was not involved on the raid of 24th July, but this was a raid of some historical significance as this was the first time that 'Window' had been dropped from bombers over Germany. I, like other airmen, had never heard of Window before; it was something completely new to us all. Window consisted of strips of metallic coated paper several inches long and a couple of inches wide. Large bundles of these strips were loaded on to the bombers and were dropped over Germany. As the bundles were dropped from the aircraft they split into single strips and floated separately to the ground. On can well imagine the problems this caused the German radar operators as the Window was showered down from hundreds of aircraft and their radar screens were swamped by radar pulses from the metal strips of paper. One wag on the squadron suggested that probably the Hun thought he was being attacked by thousands of small aircraft, a bit far-fetched but nevertheless I feel the first attack of Window must have caused panic at the German radar stations.

The main purpose of this jamming device was to hamper the activities of the German night fighters and on the first occasion it was used over Hamburg it appears to have been quite successful as only twelve crews failed to return from a total of over 700 dispatched by Bomber Command.

Number 76 Squadron lost one aircraft of the 24 dispatched on this raid. When I talked to crews after the raid, they seemed convinced from the large number of fires still burning when they left the target area that the city had been very badly damaged, especially in the area north of the Elbe where the built-up area had taken quite a pounding. One can imagine what panic reigned when after the RAF night raid, the Americans arrived with their daylight contribution.

The night after the first of this series of raids on Hamburg, Harris switched the bomber force back to the Ruhr to Essen just to remind the folks in the Valley they had not been forgotten. The squadron sent 22 aircraft and all came home safely – a good effort considering it was Essen.

I missed this raid to Essen and also the second raid to Hamburg on 27th July, but was all set for the Hamburg attack of 29th July.

We took off at 22.10 on the 29th, and it was about 01.00 on the 30th that we arrived over Hamburg to find many searchlights still very active and still plenty of flak shells exploding about the height and in the vicinity of the bomber stream. The city itself seemed to be emanating a sort of red glow as we made our bombing run on the Pathfinders' markers and as our bombs left the aircraft I felt we were just stoking up the fires that appeared to have been burning for days. I also felt sure that the casualties in this doomed city must be enormous and for those still alive it must be hell upon earth, but was soon thinking of our own survival again as a Halifax passed just under our nose.

On the way home there appeared to be some night fighters about, but we did not have to fire a shot in anger and they did

76 Squadron aircrew and transport just before take-off. The pilot leaning against the lorry's front wing is believed to be Flight Lieutenant R.A.M. Lemmon who was killed right at the end of his tour when he was shot down on operations to Düsseldorf, 22/23rd April 1944.

76 Squadron Halifax Vs at Holme-on-Spalding Moor in 1943

not fire at us, so it was over the North Sea and back to base arriving about 04.00. Some 23 aircraft of 76 Squadron had taken part, but one had failed to return so as usual I hoped that the crew had escaped the 'Reaper'.

The city of Hamburg was still on my mind when I awoke just before midday and after dressing made my way to the sergeants' mess where I was to find that our crew was once again on the battle order with briefing scheduled for 19.30 hours. The crew were not complaining about having to operate on successive nights as, like myself, they all wanted to get on with the job and finish our tour. Now that we were over the halfway mark to the magic 30, there was a feeling that we were on the home stretch.

The target turned out to be Remscheid, so once again it was back to the Ruhr. Remscheid was one of the smaller industrial Ruhr towns lying south-east of Düsseldorf, near Wuppertal, so we were quite familiar with the area and had a fair idea what defences to expect. No matter in which direction we approached Ruhr targets there always seemed to be cones of searchlights, light flak, heavy flak, box barrage flak and anything else they could throw at us.

As usual we weaved our way through the defences and over the target, where we were able to pick up the Pathfinder target indicators and make a decent bombing run despite the intensive Ack-Ack barrage. I could pick up some ground detail as we bombed and it appeared to me that the attack was striking home around the area marked by the Pathfinders. It took between ten and fifteen minutes and that seemed an eternity to weave our way out of the concentrated barrage. Then I kept my fingers crossed that a night fighter would not pounce on us. It was all speed for the Dutch coast and the quiet of the North Sea still keeping a look out for Hun fighter aircraft waiting to pick off the bomber straying outside the main stream, then the great sight of the British coast as we crossed to comparative safety, landing at 03.40 on 31st July. This was to be our last operational sortie in July and out of 20 squadron aircraft involved one failed to return – pity everyone did not get back safely, but that's war.

On 2nd August 1943, Harris sent the bomber force back to

Hamburg for a final onslaught on the important naval, military and industrial target. He certainly intended to make sure that this city would not contribute very much towards the German war effort for some time to come. Taking off at 23.15 hours we were over the enemy coast at about 01.20 and making for a final turning point about 40 miles south of Hamburg. The weather conditions we were encountering were foul with large amounts of cumulo nimbus streaking across the sky, giving very strong winds with showers of rain and hail and the sky being lit with great flashes of lightning. I thought conditions might improve but instead they got worse the nearer we got to the turning point.

We were now in a very violent electric storm with some parts of the aircraft appearing to be surrounded by haloes of fire. All very frightening and I had never experienced anything like this before or since. The most frightening part of this storm was the hazard of clear icing which was forming very rapidly on the leading edges of the wings and on the control surfaces. I knew that we could not survive in these conditions very long as the aircraft controls were sure to be affected as they became iced up.

Just at this time George was beginning to feel the effect on his controls and we had to move quickly to escape, so the bomb doors were opened and we released our load and started altering course to avoid the storm and get back on a track that would take us to our homeward exit point on the enemy coast. It was wonderful to escape from this exceptionally severe electrical storm and I was pleased to see the ice disappearing from the airframe.

In no way could we have made the target under these circumstances, but I was a bit sorry about this, as up to now we had a 100% record of reaching the target. On the way home I had a thought about this raid and felt that perhaps the Great God in his wisdom had decided the city of Hamburg had suffered enough and had sent the storm to save its inhabitants any further suffering. It is interesting to note that the code name Operation 'Gomorrah' was used for this series of operations on Hamburg.

On arrival back at base we found that most crews had to abandon the raid without getting to the target. A few managed to get through and dropped their bombs on various parts of the city which was reported to have many fires burning over wide areas.

Although this final raid on Hamburg had been disrupted due to weather the other three during the previous nine days had been most successful and reconnaissance after the final raid showed that docks, shipyards, factories, workshops and housing had all taken terrible punishment. Large parts of the city lay in ruins where the high explosive bombs had blasted the buildings and incendiary bombs had caused many fires which apparently had burned for several days and caused a firestorm in the area where the fires were most intense. Many of the dead which were thought to number over 40,000 had been caught up in the effects of the firestorm.

I feel sure that the enormous damage wrought and casualties sustained by the city and population of Hamburg must have caused some great concern to the hierarchy of the Reich because raids of this magnitude must be playing havoc with the German economy.

For nearly a week after the Battle of Hamburg my mind was most active with the thoughts of how much punishment the Germans could soak up, for, make no mistake about it, Hamburg and many of the Ruhr towns and cities had been devastated and large areas of them reduced to rubble. Many thousands of the German civilian population were dead and many more thousands were injured and often homeless. In many cases industry was crippled with plant and machinery destroyed and factories burnt out shells. Even with all this there did not seem to be any sign that German morale would collapse under the onslaught. The morale of the man in the street and the whole civilian population seemed never to break, but I am sure that on many occasions it must have undergone enormous amounts of strain as the aerial bombardment reduced their towns and cities to rubble.

It must be remembered the Bosche were still occupying very

many countries in Europe and forcing the occupied peoples to work in producing arms and equipment for the German war effort. The Germans were always adept at repairing and rebuilding their own factories, workshops, plant and machinery damaged in air raids. It was quite amazing how quickly they seemed to rebuild and repair damaged equipment.

Like Sir Arthur Harris, I had at one time during the war hoped that perhaps bombing alone could see the Germans brought to their knees. However from what I had seen of the German resilience I was now convinced that this was not possible and that ultimate victory would only be achieved by the Allies' landing on the Continent and driving the enemy from all the occupied countries and then defeating him in his own homeland. To me the sooner the Allies were in a position to open a Second Front and land on the Continent the better, but I could not see this happening in 1943 and I felt the spring or early summer would be the best time to make an attack across the Channel. I was also certain that Churchill wanted to see some of the German military strength sapped by the Red Army on the Eastern Front before committing his armies against the German defences in France and the Low Countries.

I did feel at this time that every Bomber Command raid on Germany's industrial potential would make it all that much easier for the Allied armies when they landed in Europe. I do not think that any of our war leaders wanted to see a prolonged war in Europe with killing fields like the First World War, so the bombers would so weaken Germany's industrial potential that a prolonged war by the German forces would be impossible and the saving in lives would be enormous.

The 9th August 1943 was to be a red-letter-day for me as that was the day I became a commissioned officer in the RAF with the rank of pilot officer. I was proud to be an officer in the Royal Air Force, for to me I was serving in the finest air force in the world. To celebrate my promotion our crew were to carry out a raid on Mannheim. Mannheim, standing on the junction of the River Rhine and River Neckar, was a fairly large industrial city near the old historical city of Heidelberg. Once again a great relief to get away from the Ruhr and escape the Happy Valley flak barrage.

We took off at 22.40 hours and it was a quiet, uneventful trip to the target which took us about 3 hours 20 minutes. The defences of the city could be seen some way from the target with quite a number of active searchlights and a fair amount of light and heavy flak coming from Mannheim and the surrounding area. After the Ruhr it was so pleasant to make our bombing run, drop our bombs and get through the main flak area relatively quickly. The journey home was as uneventful as the trip out and we were calling up base for landing instructions at about 05.10 hours. Once again we could record another successful raid in our log books and only hoped that our remaining operations would be as easy on the nerves as this had been.

During the next couple of days George, who also had been commissioned, and myself moved from our Nissen hut accommodation and the sergeants' mess to officers' quarters and the officers' mess. After the Nissen huts with their separate wash places it was very pleasant to have one's own room with wash basin and inside toilets. The officers' mess public rooms were very much quieter places than the sergeants' mess ante-room where one often found the Canadian members of the squadron having a dice game on the middle of the floor where considerable amounts of money would change hands on the throw of the dice. It was quite entertaining to watch the game in progress as each thrower of the dice had his own peculiar way of talking to them before he threw them into the middle of the circle formed by the players sitting on the floor. The extent of my consumption of liquor amounted only to a few half pints of beer, so I never really got too involved in the big drinking parties that seemed to be a regular feature of the bar area.

I would miss the friends I had made in the sergeants' mess and the long chats and discussions we had which covered every subject from war, sport, sex to politics and pubs that served the best beer. It was always interesting to compare notes on how they had fared on a particular operation and how their morale was standing up to the battles.

82

It was always heartbreaking when some failed to return from a sortie, but these things had to be overcome and one had to put it behind him and hope that it would not be his turn next. George and I had little difficulty in settling in at the officers' mess as Reg and Joe were already commissioned, so they were able to show us the ropes and also challenged us at billiards and snooker in the games room. Now I was in the mess I hoped our luck would hold and give me some time to enjoy the advantages of officers' mess life.

One thing that really delighted me was just prior to commissioning I had gone home for a few days' leave to get my officer's uniform and kit and my folks were delighted with my promotion. I always felt so sorry for the old folks who had sons and relatives flying in Bomber Command because they knew just how desperately dangerous bomber operations could be as the daily news bulletin on the radio gave the number of aircraft missing and one did not need to be a mathematician to calculate just what were the odds for survival. I always tried to give my folks a ring on the telephone on the day after a big operation when there had been many losses just to let them know I was still hale and hearty. I feel sure those few words did much to alleviate a mother's concern, for if some dear one was missing theirs was the biggest heartbreak.

On 12th August it was the turn of Italy to receive some attention from Bomber Command and the northern industrial city of Milan was to be our target with 76 Squadron sending 22 aircraft. This was to be the longest trip of our tour, but I was quite looking forward to it as a large part of the trip would be over France and provided the Germans did not move too many fighters into the area I could not see the flak being a big problem.

Our route took us down through France to a point due west of Milan, quite near the Italian border and then it was on to an easterly course as we crossed the French–Italian border and made for Milan. All through France our flight had been so quiet that one felt it difficult to believe that we were over enemy-occupied territory. The weather was kind to us with bright moonlight. Normally we would be operating in conditions of as little moonlight as possible as this afforded the bombers greater cover, but on this occasion I was enjoying being able to pick up so much ground detail. I will never forget on our final leg to the target area, there on our port side was the Swiss border with the Alps standing out so majestic and beautiful in the moonlight I could pick out the mountains and was pretty certain I could see Mont Blanc and the Matterhorn. There on the mountainside were the small villages and hamlets with their lights flickering and the whole scene looking so very peaceful. I thought how lucky the Swiss were to be at peace and not to be involved in this bloody war, but one day it would end and perhaps, if I survived, I could visit this land with its beautiful mountain scenery.

The whole panorama set out before me will live forever in my mind as one of the greatest sights I have ever viewed from an aircraft flying at night and only wished I could have photographed this wonderful view of Switzerland and the Alps.

My views of scenic splendour were to be rudely interrupted as away ahead of us searchlights and flak were quite active. I assumed the first bombers were arriving in the target area and flares and target markers were going down on the city of Milan. As we neared the city there appeared to be much less flak than I had anticipated and the barrage was much smaller than I had witnessed just prior to reaching the target area and for this I was thankful. The searchlights seemed to be quite ineffective against the bomber stream and did not appear to be working to any particular pattern.

On arrival over Milan the target indicators appeared to be marking the area of heavy industry in the city which was receiving a pounding as the attack was pressed home and the flak barrage seemed to diminish in intensity. I remember thinking as I bombed, had the anti-aircraft gunners given up the ghost and taken shelter or perhaps they were short of shells? There is one thing for sure it did not compare with the defences of the Ruhr cities and for that we were all grateful. It was not long before we cleared their defences and settled down to what we hoped would be a quiet return journey.

I was thoroughly enjoying our homeward flight and was feeling quite pleased with myself as I was able to do some map reading by the light of the moon. The navigator suggested we might take some star shots while over Central France as things were extremely quiet with no active defences to be seen. I moved myself from the bomb aimer's compartment and armed with a sextant took a few star shots from the astro-dome at the rear of the pilot's position.

This was a clear perspex dome giving clear vision to the sky above the aircraft. Astro navigation was not the most accurate method of air navigation but crews were encouraged to practise this method in case it should be needed when other navigation aids were not available. On this occasion I passed my sextant readings to Reg who, from our air almanac and air navigation tables was able to work our position lines that gave us a fix about ten miles from our actual position which we had pinpointed a few minutes earlier, so for astro-navigation this was a fairly good result.

This was certainly a very long sortie compared to the short trips to the Ruhr. It had taken us about 4 hours 40 minutes to Milan and we reckoned it would take the same for the return journey. I was certain, like myself, the crew did not mind the length of this trip as it was so peaceful and such a wonderful night for flying. The only enemy activity that we were to experience on the homeward journey was somewhere north of Paris where night fighters were active. Night fighter flares were being dropped by the Germans in the area between Paris and the coast and it was necessary for us all to keep a good look out for any intruder penetrating the bomber stream. Our gunners were not reporting any sightings and I felt sure that the main activity was well away to the north of our track.

We passed over the French coast and made our way over the Channel towards the English coast and it was not too long before we were heading north towards the Humber and our base at Holme. We touched down at 06.15 hours after a flight of about 9 hours 20 minutes so we were a tired crew as we made our way to debriefing and a very acceptable cup of hot coffee.

We had quite an enjoyable flight so after our debriefing it was hard to believe that of the 22 aircraft from 76 Squadron dispatched, two had failed to return but it was wonderful to learn that one of the missing aircraft had landed in Algeria and was to be back with the squadron a few days later. It was always marvellous news when a crew posted missing was suddenly to turn up having cheated death and avoided the Hun.

If there was one thing this quiet raid to Milan was to teach us when we knew that a crew was missing it was that over Europe there was no easy target and there were no trouble-free routes to and from targets. In fact, there was no hiding place and only eternal vigilance and a heap of good luck would help us complete a tour of operations.

A sort of breathless hush fell over the briefing room on the evening of 17th August as the cover was removed from the briefing map at the far end of the room revealing the target to be Peenemünde, a small place on the Baltic Coast, some 50 miles north of Stettin. I suppose the reason for the hush was that none of the assembled crews had ever heard of this small place before. Everybody realized that the place must contain something that was a potential danger to our war effort as the briefing officer described the place as having research laboratories and an aircraft testing site. In actual fact this was the German V-Weapon Research Establishment.

I thought it must be important when Bomber Command were sending 600 bombers to a target not much bigger than one of our large airfields. They were sending the bombers on a moonlight night and bringing them down from the normal bombing level of about 18,000 feet to bomb at 6,000 feet. They were laying on a spoof raid by Mosquitoes to Berlin. To ensure that there would be no difficulty identifying the target and arriving on time the Pathfinders were dropping a marker on one of the off-shore islands in the Baltic so the bombers could carry out a timed run into Peenemünde.

If anything else was needed to convince us of the importance of this raid we were informed should this establishment not be destroyed then we would return again and again until such time as it was. It was with the importance of this operation on our minds that we took off at 20.50 hours. It was a beautiful night and the moon was shining brightly as we made the long flight over the North Sea, over Denmark and into the Baltic. The weather was wonderfully clear as we cruised above the waters of the Baltic and had little difficulty in picking up and identifying the coloured marker on the off-shore island of Roden. We made a turn over the marker on to a southerly course for our final run in on the target which was now being marked by the Pathfinders. As we got nearer I could see lots of explosions on the ground and bombs crashing through the buildings. On our own bombing run I could see what I believed to be the workshop buildings and nearby buildings that looked like living accommodation, but at a height of 6,000 feet it was all coming at me so very quickly and in no time at all with a few:

'Left, Left,'

'Steady,'

instructions with our bomb doors open, the aiming point was tracking down the centre line on my bombsight reflector plate and on reaching the release point it was;

'Bombs gone,'

and as the bombs dropped from the fuselage it was:

'Bomb Doors closed,'

as I watched our bombs crash down on the buildings below. It was at this point the nose of our aircraft came up very rapidly and was to give me a bit of shake as I wondered if we had been hit as there was quite a lot of flak about, but not as much as I expected. As it turned out, we had not been hit and probably the noselift was due to our bombing level of 6,000 feet where it was quite possible that vibrations from the bombs hitting the ground had caused the sudden uplift. The flak in the target area in my estimation was only moderate to slight and considering we were at 6,000 feet, I was surprised we did not encounter much more light flak which was usually active up to about 8,000 feet.

As we turned away from the now blasted and burning buildings it was obvious to everyone that this had been a particularly well planned and executed attack. The concentration of bombs on the target was as good as I had seen any-where. The Pathfinders had done a good job with their markers on the target and on the island of Roden for the timed run.

On leaving the Peenemünde area it quickly became apparent that there were a large number of German fighter aircraft about and were attacking the homeward-bound bombers. Hundreds of night fighter flares were being dropped along the route of the bombers. These flares with the aid of the moonlight were making the bombers sitting targets for the fighters. I had never felt so exposed to the fighters as I did on this occasion as conditions were ideal for picking out and shooting down intruding aircraft so I was not surprised that George felt the same way as he kept warning the crew to be on the alert for fighters.

We were once again lucky enough to avoid the fighter pilots but believe that some of the later waves of bombers were to experience fierce fighter attacks from what appeared to have been a late concentrated effort by many fighters to destroy as many bombers as possible in a clear moonlit sky which was ideal for their operations.

The weather continued good as we sped over the North Sea bound for old England's shore. About half way across the sea it was discovered that we had a hydraulic leak and this was a bit worrying, so after a bit of discussion with Ferris, our flight engineer, George, decided that as we neared the English coast our wireless operator would report our predicament and request base for landing instructions. The result of our request was that we were ordered to land at Wymeswold, a wartime airfield near Loughborough in Leicestershire. Reg was quick to work out our new course and we were soon overhead at Wymeswold receiving landing instructions and coming in to land about 04.30 hours.

The crew were not too pleased at having to stay overnight away from base. However under the circumstances there was little else we could do. Joe released the two pigeons that we always carried with a message to base that we hoped to be home soon – a bit naughty of him as these birds were only to be used in an emergency, but Joe's story was that they needed a practice flight.

We found that our aircraft would require some quite complicated servicing and it was likely to remain at Wymeswold for a few days, so at 14.30 hours, Sergeant Wright arrived in a 76 Squadron Halifax and we all piled on board and were transported back to Holme on Spalding Moor. It was nice to get back to one's own base and to be welcomed by the old faces and to find that all the squadron crews were back safe and sound after Peenemünde.

At our small debriefing we found that most crews had thought that the raid on this Baltic Research Centre had been a complete success and like ourselves, thought that there would be very little left standing and it was most unlikely that we would have to give a repeat performance. The proof of the pudding would have to wait till after the Photographic Reconnaissance flights had confirmed our success.

An attack of this type cannot be carried out without casualties and although I expected we would have losses, I never dreamed that 40 of our aircraft would fail to return out of the 597 dispatched. For once 76 Squadron had been lucky with all aircraft back safely, so I sincerely hoped that this lucky trend would continue.

The destruction of Peenemünde had been a must and as the story of the V-Weapon establishment unfolded it was not surprising that Sir Arthur Harris had sent nearly 600 bombers to completely saturate and destroy such a small but extremely dangerous target.

Churchill and his Chiefs of Staff had been most concerned at Intelligence Reports they were receiving about a German secret weapon being produced, perfected and tested at the Peenemünde Research Centre on the Baltic.

The weapon was being described as an unmanned rocket filled with high explosives and from sightings could fly at supersonic speeds and was believed to have a range of well over one hundred miles, making it possible for it to reach London and the main towns and cities of Southern England from launching pads in France.

This was most disturbing to Winston Churchill and it made

him furious when he thought of Great Britain and the civilian population having to suffer a further blitz on their cities with unmanned rockets which to his way of thinking was not quite cricket; at one time he secretly thought of retaliation with gas attacks but was deterred from pursuing this course of action by his Chiefs of Staff.

This raid was a great success and Bomber Command were never to return to this establishment. Our leaders must have breathed a sigh of relief as in the short term this raid had delayed the launching of V-Weapons on England, but for how long no one was quite certain.

As it worked out in the long term, the Germans were to fire nearly 10,000 V1 and V2 weapons into southern England, the majority of them being targeted on the London area.

I only hoped that the aircrew who had failed to return and had died on the Peenemünde raid had not made this sacrifice in vain because their efforts in delaying the V-Weapon attacks on British cities had saved many thousands of British lives.

After 21 sorties our crew were now on the last third of our tour and were beginning to think we were within sight of our objective, but funnily enough at this stage of the tour each operation seemed to be more and more difficult to face up to, as one's luck had been so wonderfully good one wondered how long it could last. It was never far from my mind that one well predicted anti-aircraft shell hitting an aircraft in the most vulnerable place could end it all.

During this particular period in the squadron there seemed to be quite a bit of anxiety in several crews and this was not surprising as our losses, perhaps not as many as some other squadrons, had been considerable during June and July, a period that included the Battle of the Ruhr and the Battle of Hamburg which had involved many large and dangerous raids on well defended targets. Each sortie was a separate battle for survival over the night skies of Germany and this fight for survival did not end till 30 operational sorties had been completed.

No two raids were ever the same and often on occasions when

one returned from a sortie and thought the ground defences or the fighter activity had not been too frightening it was sobering to find that perhaps one or two aircraft from the squadron had failed to return and on listening to the radio next day, hearing that maybe 20 or 30 of our aircraft were missing. There was no way that anyone in his right mind would ever believe that chances or liberties could be taken while over Germany and the occupied countries.

I would not have anyone believe that aircrew tended to dwell on what some thought was their forthcoming doom. In fact in many cases the opposite would apply where many would do everything possible and in some cases, the nigh impossible, to ensure that if they were doomed to be shot down over Europe they would have spent what time they had left on the squadron enjoying themselves and doing the things that they enjoyed doing most. In off-duty periods many, like myself, would try and forget what the next briefing would throw up.

I remember one afternoon while reading a newspaper in the officers' mess ante-room I was approached by the station padre who introduced himself to me. As we were the only two in the room at this time, he sat down and started to chat to me and after a few minutes I was amazed to find he knew more about me than I had guessed as he obviously had been speaking to other members of my crew. He knew us to be a closely knit crew and one of the longer-serving crews on 76 Squadron. We chatted for the best part of an hour and I was most impressed with this man who was Church of England and had bothered to come and speak to me, a Church of Scotland man. He was very knowledgeable about Scotland and I believe pre-war had spent quite a lot of holidays north of the border. He was a man in his late forties who, with this little chinwag, had raised my spirits by assuring me that he felt sure our crew would finish a tour of operations. Often a casual meeting like this or a good old natter with some of the other squadron officers would help one to forget the war.

Sport had always played a big part in my young life and on afternoons when we were free from operations that night, Reg,

George, myself and a few others would take to the football field and enjoy a game of soccer followed by a shower and a few beers in the mess bar and always found this wonderful relaxation.

I never did find a golf course in this area, so had to content myself knocking a few balls about on a grass strip near our living quarters. It was not a very long strip of grass, but was sufficient for the Number 5 Iron I kept handy.

I had many chats with the Norwegian, Canadian, Australian and other Commomwealth officers on the station who, although a very long way from home, were always so full of high spirits. The Norwegian boys were very friendly but had a very great hatred for the Germans and were living for the day when the Hun could be driven out of their land and they could return to their 'Ain Folk' and I only hoped that this would be in the near future.

Leverkusen, one of the smaller towns a few miles north of Cologne on the east bank of the Rhine, possessed chemical works which Harris thought required the attention of his bombers, and he dispatched them there on 22nd August. Some 22 aircraft from 76 Squadron took part. We had a straightforward trouble-free trip outward-bound until approaching the Cologne area where the usual Ruhr firework display was encountered. On this occasion we had the luxury of large amounts of cloud which was protecting us from the glare of searchlights, but did not prevent the heavy flak from reaching the level of the bomber stream, to scare the daylights out of one as it started to get too near for comfort.

The cloud cover meant that ground marking was not possible so Pathfinder Force used the Wanganui sky marking technique. I felt it a pity that we had been unable to get a view of the place as ground marking by PFF was always much more accurate. However, weather conditions could not always be accurately forecast and often sky marking had to suffice.

The homeward journey produced no problems after breaking free from the Ruhr. On arrival at base we found after debriefing that all the squadron aircraft had returned safely. I was to feel that this was not one of Bomber Command's better raids as if the aiming points we were endeavouring to strike had been hit I felt this would be due more to saturation bombing rather than accurate aiming. However, the results would only be known when photo reconnaissance had been carried out. As it so happened a few days later reconnaissance reports confirmed that the raid had not been a great success as the chemical works which had been our main objective, were still in operation. It must be remembered that often the success or failure of raids like this was very much dependent upon favourable weather conditions.

On 23rd August, it was at the early evening briefing we were to find that at 20.00 hours that night we would be on our way to the 'Big City', Berlin. We had never been there before but we had heard many very frightening stories about the strength of the city defences. I suppose I should have felt afraid but did not seem to feel so. Perhaps this was because we had already faced the fury of Essen, Cologne, Hamburg, and all the shells the Ruhr gunners could pump into the night sky. My own view was that Berlin would have to resemble hell if their defences were to be more concentrated than those experienced in and around the city of Essen.

One thing that did worry me was that the round flight would take about eight hours and quite a number of hours would be spent over German territory where their night fighter force would have plenty of time to track us down. The weather forecast was for good weather with no moon to show us up in the night sky so this would help, although the Germans could be depended upon to lay many night fighter flares to light up the bomber stream. I tried to console myself by thinking that because this was such a large raid with about 700 bombers taking part that this would do much to swamp the defences.

The whole crew were obviously a bit apprehensive about a flight of this sort especially so far on in our tour and I could sense a tenseness just before take-off (always the worst time), but felt this would soon be overcome when we got airborne.

The route to Berlin was quite straightforward and for once quite direct. It was over the sea to Holland and practically due

93

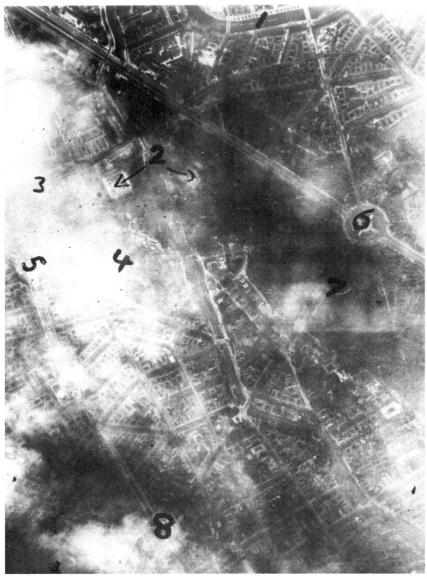

Berlin, eight hours after the attack on 23/24 August 1943. *Key:* 1. River Spree, 2. Two flak towers, anti-aircraft guns mounted – a characteristic feature of German AA defences. 3. Zoo Station. 4. Auguste Viktoria Platz. 5. Grosse Stern. 6. Tiergarten. 7. Hollendorf Platz.

east keeping north of Hanover and then on past Wolfsburg, heading for the German capital. We were on one of the early waves and were certainly not having any trouble along our outward route. Perhaps the Germans had not yet worked out which city we were about to attack, but it would not take them long to figure it all out.

As we approached within about 30 miles of the city there appeared to be a very large number of active searchlights, some were acting singly, some in twos and threes, then there were large cones of perhaps ten or twelve clustered round a master blue searchlight. The master blue was obviously being radar predicted on to the bombers so that the others in the cone could follow. Just ahead of these appeared to be some large flashes and it looked as if some of our bombers were in trouble. Over the city the Pathfinders were dropping their illuminating flares and fairly quickly afterwards these were followed by red and green target indicators cascading down on to our aiming point in the city.

We were now over the outskirts and as the Ack-Ack shells started to arrive in ever increasing numbers, they were everywhere. I could see them bursting to port, to starboard and what looked like hundreds just below us. I could also see many of our own bombers very near us as they were caught in the light of the searchlights. I was trying the best I could to direct George through the field of flak that lay ahead of us, but at this time there seemed very little room for manoeuvring as there seemed to be shells bursting everywhere. As we headed towards the target markers burning brightly in huge coloured blobs on the ground in the built-up area, it was time to look through the bombsight and request:

'Bomb Doors open', and George repeated:

'Bomb Doors open.'

I started guiding George with:

'Left, Left.'

'Steady.'

'Right.'

'Steady.'

directions which brought the markers down the centre line of my bombsight and as soon as they reached the release point on the sighting head I called:

'Bombs gone',

as I pressed hard on the bomb release button and watched the bombs fall from the aircraft fuselage and called for bomb doors to be closed and George confirmed:

'Bomb doors closed.'

As I looked at the aiming point and the city below we seemed to be passing over crescents of streets with hundreds upon hundreds of houses with, just ahead, larger buildings where the main attack seemed to be centred and where the haze from the fires and bombs exploding seemed to be obscuring the buildings. The impression I had in my mind was that the houses I had seen were workers' houses and the larger buildings were factories and workshops. While admiring this view and reporting to George of my sightings the voice of Reg, our navigator, came through the intercom saying with some anxiety:

'Let's drop the bombs and let's get to f—— out of this place.'

The Ack-Ack shells were still thick and heavy and I was not quite sure how we could get through the city without being hit, but I kept trying to find a way through this massive flak field. Just at this time the flight engineer reported a night fighter passing overhead. I remember thinking:

'That's all we need.'

The scene set out below me was one I will never forget. On the ground there were now several green target indicators nestling near the original reds which had now dimmed quite considerably. There were large and small explosions all over the city as the high explosive bombs struck at the buildings. There were large and small fires, like a mosaic covering large parts of the city. From the ground up to our flight level there must have been hundreds of anti-aircraft shells, all exploding about the same time and I did not like the large and small explosions that were occurring about the level of the bomber stream which were probably aircraft being hit. One very large explosion slightly below us and off to starboard, frightened me with its intensity and the thought crossed my mind that it could have been two bombers crashing into each other. However, we were not near enough to confirm this or to see any parachutes that might have come out of the explosion. We looked as if we were through the worst of the flak as Reg passed the new course to George and it was home, Skipper, and don't spare the revs.

As we looked back at the target area, the raid was still going strong but what we were now concerned with was the danger of a night fighter attack because we knew them to be active and sure to be awaiting the bombers leaving the target.

Our route home was fairly direct and although there were some fighter flares and obviously quite a lot of activity, the gunners had no sightings and we were to appreciate an uneventful quiet journey to the coast and over the North Sea. Just as we approached the English Coast Jock, our wireless operator, received a radio message instructing us to land at RAF Catfoss. I did not like this diversion too much, but after what we had been through I would settle for any friendly airfield. We landed just after 04.00 and how wonderful to be back safe and sound and how very happy the crew looked as they sat there eating a hearty breakfast. This had been one of the largest raids by heavy bombers to the German capital, but raids like these are not without casualties and 58 aircraft of the 700 dispatched were missing.

Joe, our mid upper gunner, ensured that Holme on Spalding Moor knew we were safe as he released the two pigeons we carried for emergencies as he reckoned they needed more flying practice.

I wondered how many casualties they were counting in the city of Berlin. I only hoped that we would not be returning, as one visit was one too many and the 'Reaper' was too active for my liking.

Berlin was to be our crew's last raid in August 1943 and we were to have a few days' break before our next operational sortie. It was quite nice to look forward to a few days' leave every six weeks while on an operational squadron. This was one of the little perks enjoyed by operational aircrew provided they could survive. It certainly needed a complete break like this to allow the jangled nerves a bit of respite and to let the mind refresh itself for the next onslaught on Hitler's Reich.

One factor that seemed to be coming up alarmingly in my mind was that George Dunn, my pilot, would complete his tour of 30 operations after three more raids and by that time Reg, our navigator, and myself would have completed only 26. Now the big question was would we be required to complete another four raids with another crew or would our 26 raids constitute a tour. Reg and I certainly hoped so, but we were prepared to do four more if required. We would only get to know the answer to this question nearer George's final trip.

On 27th August our crew were not involved on the Nuremberg raid but the squadron dispatched 24 aircraft. One aircraft was missing, that being the one with Flight Sergeant Ward and crew. Although any of our aircrew missing always received my sympathy, on this occasion the navigator, Flying Officer Peter Carling, had been one of my friends for some time and I sadly missed him in the mess. This was the thing that would tug at the heartstrings and I only hoped that he had survived and perhaps if he had not escaped, he was a POW.

It was some considerable time after that I was to find that he had died in the skies over Germany. It was sometimes very difficult to realize that they had gone and would not be returning.

It was news like this that tended to be so upsetting when the end of a tour seemed to be in sight, for here was a young man, the same age as myself (21), with his whole life before him, being cut down in his prime. It did not bear thinking about how many had gone and how many more would go before this bloody war was over. I said a little prayer and hoped the Good Lord was on our side for we certainly needed help considering the losses of Bomber Command aircrew.

It was the battle order of 6th September that showed Pilot Officer Dunn and crew back on the operation scene, so it was briefing late that afternoon. It appeared with such an early briefing, that it would be a long sortie and we were not disappointed as the briefing map showed the route tapes all the way across to Munich. Pre-war I had always dreamed of visiting Bavaria and Austria, but never dreamed that a Halifax bomber would be my means of transportation.

Munich, the heartland of Hitler and the Nazi Party, a large industrial city with many factories and workshops, both large and small, producing a great variety of weapons, equipment and goods to help fuel the German war machine. The city had first been bombed by the RAF in September 1942 and as recently as March 1943, but no doubt during the last few months, factories, plant and machinery would have been repaired and would be sure to be producing again.

The long haul over enemy territory or occupied territory was always worrying as fighters were sure to be operating along our tracks both on the outward and return journeys.

We took off at 19.00 hours and arrived in the target area about 23.15 hours. The gunners had reported a couple of fighters enroute but we slipped past them unnoticed or perhaps they were too involved chasing some other bomber. There was quite a large number of searchlights very active in and around the city and the defences were throwing up a great amount of flak but we weaved our way in towards the target marker burning on the ground and had a fairly straightforward, revs up, nose down run through the target with bombs, I believed, falling on the area marked by the Pathfinders.

Looking down, there appeared lots of fire tracks and explosions on the ground, lots of shells bursting about our level, but we had no hits and it was alter course for the United Kingdom and everybody looking and alert for the dreaded fighters.

Everything went as per plan until we reached the English Coast when our wireless operator picked up a message diverting us to Harland Bridge where we landed at 03.35. We were all pleased to be back safe and sound but wanted to get back to Holme as soon as possible. Unfortunately we had a lot of hanging around before we took off at 10.30 for Holme and by lunchtime that day all the crew were pleased to get their heads down and catch up with our sleep.

The tension was quite apparent on the faces of our crew as we attended the mid-afternoon briefing on 3rd October, for this was to be the final operational sortie of our tour. My eyes never moved from the briefing map as the cover was removed revealing the target to be Kassel. First impression 'Well, thank goodness it's not the Ruhr' and I am sure the others in the crew agreed wholeheartedly. Kassel was an important manufacturing and industrial city about 130 miles due east of Düsseldorf on the River Fulda in the southern part of the Rheinhordswald Region. The city was known to be an important rail junction in that area and had many factories and workshops directly involved in supplying weapons for the German armed forces. The Feisler aircraft factory was producing FW 190 fighter aircraft for the Luftwaffe. Other factories were producing Tiger tanks and anti-tank weapons for the Wehrmacht. Smaller establishments were producing equipment and spares for mechanical vehicles and a rail workshop was turning out locomotives.

The impetus of production of these factories was greatly assisted by the thousands of forced labour personnel imported from the occupied countries, so we hoped they would not be at the receiving end when our bombs crashed onto the city. The place was known to Bomber Command as it had been first visited in August 1942.

We would be taking off in daylight at 18.00 hours and all being well Reg calculated we should be touching down back at base at 40 minutes after midnight. As Reg and I drew up the tracks on our maps he whispered to me:

'Well, Andy, this is the last, so don't let's spend too much time in the target area. We want to be home a bit earlier tonight.'

There was some happy chatter and a fair amount of tension and I felt a bit more edgy than usual as we sat outside our bombed-up aircraft having a cigarette and awaiting our take off time. I just wanted to get into the aircraft and get airborne so I could busy myself and get my mind off things.

When we did start to roll along the perimeter track towards the runway in use, I was quite surprised to see a number of our

Flight Lieutenant Jimmy Steele (who died from injuries received in a flying accident on 3rd November 1943) prepares to take off from Holme-on-Spalding Moor for the raid on Kassel on 22nd October 1943. His Halifax B.V DK168 MP-H is being waved away by (left to right) Johny Waldo, RNAF, Major John Stene, RNAF, Squadron Leader Nigel Bennett, Flight Lieutenant Turner, 'Pop' Bligh the squadron adjutant, and 'The Colonel' the squadron's intelligence officer.

Karlsruhe under fire — note the TIs cascading top left

squadron friends who had taken up position near the control caravan at the end of the runway. How very nice of them to come along and wave us off on our final raid. It did make us feel good. I remember thinking to myself as I climbed down into the bomb aimer's compartment after take off, if we could survive the next 6 hours 40 minutes our tour would be complete and the pressure would be off.

The weather was good and we had a completely uneventful flight to the target where we arrived about 21.15 hours to find the Pathfinders had the place lit up and I could see from some distance off the green target indicators cascading down on the city. As we weaved our way on towards the aiming point the searchlights and flak were a bit troublesome but nothing like what I had expected. George had the revs up and the nose slightly down as we headed for the green markers which were now on the ground and burning brightly. It was time to open the bomb doors, then it was:

'Left, Left, Steady,'

'Steady,'

'Right a little,'

'Steady,'

The green target indicators were moving down the centre line of the bombsight and it was:

'Hold it there. Steady,'

as they reached the release point. It was:

'Bombs Gone,' then

'Bomb Doors Closed,'

'Weave to Starboard.'

I watched our bombs go down towards the target markers in the built-up area of the city. My heart was thumping away as I watched some anti-aircraft shells exploding a little below our aircraft and it was:

'Keep weaving, George,'

as the searchlights swept across the night sky just ahead of us. With nose down and revs up we were soon clearing the main defences of the city and as we altered course I looked back at the aiming point and in the haze of burning fires, large and small, the high explosive bombs were blasting the built-up area and it looked a very successful raid. I thought if we could get home safely this would be the last target I would be looking at for some time to come. Reg passed the new course to George and he turned the aircraft for home and I was beginning to think we were on the home stretch, but was still thinking of the lurking fighter which could attack us anywhere along our homeward route, so it was all eyes searching for the Hun in the night sky.

George, on this occasion, was not sparing the power and it was hell for leather towards the enemy coast and across the North Sea, back to Holme on Spalding Moor. It was not surprising we were the first aircraft home and as we got permission to land immediately, touching down at 35 minutes past midnight. As George braked and the aircraft came to a stop at the end of our landing run a great cheer rang out over the intercommunication system. A cheer for George who was a great pilot and a great captain; also the cheer was one of relief and great joy that we had survived a tour of operations and as I stepped from the aircraft I felt like kissing the ground.

I think it was only after debriefing when Don Smith, our squadron commander, congratulated us and assured me that I would not require to do a further four operations to complete my 30 as I was now deemed to have completed my tour, that I realized that I would no longer have to dice with death over Germany at least for the time being.

What a great feeling of elation! One felt the Reaper had laid down his scythe and given up trying to cut us down. We had survived against the odds. I remember thinking I better ring my folks and let them know I had finished and this I did before starting on a celebration and series of parties that was to last for about a week. I remember being brought down to earth suddenly as someone told us that four of our squadron aircraft were missing. I was quite stunned by the news as we had never lost four aircraft in any one sortie during our time with 76 Squadron. When I came to turn into bed about five in the morning, even if I had been drinking, my thoughts turned to the

28 boys from the squadron we had left behind in Germany and I prayed somehow they would survive.

The week after completing our tour, between the parties and celebration I got to thinking how very much I would miss the comradeship of our crew because soon we would all be posted to different training establishments as instructors. We had been a closely knit crew enjoying each other's company and sharing the many trials and tribulations of service life. I only hoped that perhaps when the war was over and peace once more returned to these islands that we could all meet together and renew our friendships.

I will always think myself privileged to have been a member of George Dunn's crew, for to me this crew had everything required to make them an efficient operational crew. They were well disciplined, worked well together as a team while on operations. They never shirked the task set them and often forced home their attack against the fiercest of defences. The camaraderie that was to be born in the heat of battle exists to this day. All of them were brave men as all operational aircrew were brave men and they all knew the survival odds stacked against them. I will always feel honoured to have been associated with this crew and thankful that we were the lucky ones for many thousands of equally brave and efficient aircrew whose luck ran out lay dead in the battlefields of Europe.

During our period of service with 76 Squadron from 23rd May 1943 till our final raid on 3rd October 1943, the squadron had taken part in the Battle of the Ruhr, the Battle of Hamburg and had started on the Battle of Berlin, so we were in every way on a front line squadron. 76 had been involved during this period on 40 bomber operations flying about 802 sorties, which meant an average of 20 aircraft on each operation.

Some 28 aircraft had failed to return and 203 aircrew were missing and although it was hoped that many might survive I had an awful feeling that a very large number were dead. Our squadron losses were high though not as many as some other squadrons, but one always tended to take one's own squadron in isolation instead of looking at the overall picture.

There was little doubt that Bomber Command was having to pay dearly for the Battles over the Ruhr, Hamburg and now Berlin. The summer of 1943 which included the Ruhr Battles threw up some frightening losses and at one stage only about 10% of crews starting a tour of operations had any chance of survival. This was certainly war at its ugliest but the spirit and morale of aircrew were magnificent.

Now our tour was at an end our memories would be with us for ever. German cities under bombardment with huge built-up areas burning and high explosives exploding, giving the effect of hell having opened up and spread its fire upon the face of the earth. Remembering next day that when the aerial pictures were taken by the reconnaissance aircraft that large parts would be shown as having been reduced to rubble and probably a large number of the citizens no longer alive. Those who were still alive struggling to repair and rebuild the important parts of their city and the morale of the population never breaking. It was always interesting to note when we had to revisit a city just how much rebuilding had taken place and I often wondered how much forced labour from the occupied countries was involved in the reconstruction programme.

I felt sure that many aircrew finishing a tour would have liked to have learned more of what exactly they had achieved during their operations, but as all the results of bombing raids could only be assessed from reconnaissance and aerial photography and sometimes with the best photography that was available at this time, it was not always possible to get sufficient detail to give us a complete picture of the target area. Often it would not be possible to say that such and such a factory or workshop had ceased to function, so the results of aerial bombardment could not always be confirmed conclusively.

The other very large imponderable question was just how much damage was being wrought on German industry by the continuous bombing of their work force because the destruction of their homes, factories, workshops and the complete thromboses of their traffic systems must have accounted for the loss of many thousand man hours at the work benches. Large numbers of workers would be required to move the rubble, clear the casualties, open the streets so traffic could move freely. All the disorganization of the labour force must have taken its toll, but still the Germans seemed to continue producing the weapons for their troops in the front line. There was one thing for certain, the German civilian population were having the horrors of war brought home to them in a manner they would not easily forget and their casualties must have been enormous.

Nineteen forty-three had been a great year for Sir Arthur Harris as he had watched Bomber Command go from strength to strength and by the summer with many more heavy bombers reaching the front line squadrons and the Commonwealth Aircrew Training Scheme now turning out thousands of aircrew, he was able to mount raids of 500, 600, 700 and sometimes more to keep smashing the German towns and cities. Harris had become well known throughout Britain; at this time his popularity was probably only second to Winston Churchill, although many stories are told of the Commander-in-Chief's harsh treatment of staff officers and how he always thought himself to be right and hated anyone to disagree with him. There is little doubt he was a ruthless commander and believed wholeheartedly that by the continuous mass area bombing of German towns and cities, he could so weaken the German ability to fight war that they would be forced to surrender to the aerial bombardment. He hoped he would so weaken their economy and ability to produce materials of war that the Allied armies would have no difficulty advancing very quickly with the minimum of casualties when they landed in Europe and moved towards Germany.

Harris was a great war leader and believed wholeheartedly in his overall strategy for the Bomber Force he so ably commanded. In the latter years of the war Harris was to disagree on many occasions with his superiors, especially when they gave top priority in the bomber offensive to all-out attacks on oil, ball bearings, communications or some other panacea targets as he called them. Harris was never keen at any time to divert much of the bomber force from his primary aim of area bombing of cities, so on occasions when he was forced to provide aircraft and crews for panacea targets he did it grudgingly and then it would be only small numbers of his main force.

On occasions due to his complete dedication to mass bombing he had many differences and arguments and sometimes came very near to being insubordinate when dealing with his superiors regarding the priorities to be given to certain types of targets.

The majority of aircrew in the front line squadrons only knew Harris by name, but to them he was their Commander-in-Chief and the Great Man from whom they took their orders. They knew he was a man who would fight for the best aircraft, equipment and conditions for his men on the operational squadrons, for he knew the odds that were staked against them.

By October 1943 it was pretty obvious that Churchill and the Allied leaders did not intend the Second Front to start till the spring of 1944 at the earliest, so in the British Isles it was the night bomber offensive by the RAF and the daylight bomber raids by the US Eighth Army Air Force that would allow the Allied armies this extra period of preparation.

During this period the folks in these British Islands were most enthusiastic about the bomber offensive and each day the Radio News would be cheered as it gave the details of the previous night's raids. In the factories, workshops, work places, pubs, clubs and in the home, the name of 'Butch' Harris and Bomber Command were to become well known as the raids became larger and larger and struck harder and harder at the German homeland. These raids without a doubt at this time were a great booster to the British morale and it was little wonder that Sir Arthur Harris was such a popular leader.

CHAPTER VII

Lichfield

It was about the middle of October 1943 that our crew had to say goodbye to 76 Squadron, to Holme on Spalding Moor and to each other as we all headed for our new stations. I was on my way to 27 Operational Training Unit at RAF Lichfield to take up instructional duties. On arrival at RAF Lichfield I was to find the airfield was only a few miles from the city of Lichfield on flat ground surrounded by gently rolling country-side and from my first impression looked a lot less bleak than Holme on Spalding Moor. This station was catering for the operational training of Australian aircrew, prior to their posting to operational squadrons.

The station was commanded by an Australian group captain and I was to find that RAF officers were very much in the minority in the mess. However the gentleman I would be working for was an RAF squadron leader, who was Chief Ground Instructor, by the name of Humphrey Foster. Humphrey was an extremely friendly fellow and pre-war was quite a well known jockey and prior to coming to Lichfield had completed a tour of operations on Pathfinder Force.

Although I had never instructed before I was thrown in at the deep end to learn very quickly the best way to impart my words of wisdom to our Australian cousins. Australian aircrew were not much different from RAF aircrew but tended to be very high-spirited, so life in the mess was never dull. At lectures they were most attentive and keen to learn and always prepared to pass a joke and see the lighter side of life. I liked instructing them and when they called me a Pommie I would tell them to crawl in their pouches. In the evenings all roads led to Lichfield and all the hotel bars and pubs were their targets. Often on occasions the landlords of these establishments would have great difficulty in controlling the high spirits of the young Australians especially when they had a little too much to drink and would get up to all sorts of tricks.

I remember on one occasion a landlord was getting a bit irate about after time drinking and the Aussies were not liking his tirade very much, so a few chairs were being broken and used as firewood in the lounge fire and one young flying officer was being restrained as he moved in to move the clock from the mantelshelf towards the burning embers, a more mature voice was saying, 'That's not cricket, old man.'

On one occasion a pub in town was broken up so badly that the police had to intervene and when the Station Commander got to know about this ugly sortie he cancelled all leave for one week till the culprits owned up and agreed to pay for the damage, but for these wild men from down under this sort of thing was just a great big joke.

I always remembered the Aussies were a long way from home and I was prepared to make excuses for them, for they had come a long way to help to fight our war. I always admired their guts, their happy go lucky nature and their earnest desire to knock hell out of the Germans. The thought that made me a little sad was that a large number of them were not likely to see Australia again.

The life for me at Lichfield was very easy going as I was only required to instruct for a few periods each day, so I volunteered as Messing Officer on the Officers' Mess Committee. This was to take me on a visit to the markets in Birmingham at least once a week. I was also given the job of supervising the practice bombing range on Lord Lichfield's ground at Cannock Chase. This meant a weekly visit to the NCOs and airmen who manned the quadrants which measured the practice bombing results. By the time Christmas 1943 came along I was quite settled at Lichfield and managed a few days' leave to visit the folks in Scotland.

Soon after the New Year I was off to No 1 Air Armament School at Manby in Lincolnshire where I was to do an Air Bomber Instructor's Course. The course lasted nearly a month and I was to enjoy it very much especially the comforts of the very fine pre-war officers' mess. In the main the classroom instruction was on bombs and their components, various bombsights and their workings, bombing theory and instruction technique. The flying side of the course was in Blenheim aircraft and consisted of about ten hours flying, mainly on exercises with different kinds of bombsights, both high level and low level. It was interesting but I did not particularly like the very old aircraft. I left Manby probably much better equipped to carry out my job as an instructor at Lichfield.

Early in February 1944, soon after my return from Manby, I was to receive information that I had been awarded the DFC and also to find that several others in our crew had been decorated. This came as quite a surprise to me, especially so long after completing our tour. I felt very, very humble and also a little proud because we were the lucky ones to survive and to be able to accept this great honour.

At the beginning of June I was once again off to Manby, this time on a Bombing Leaders' Course. The course was of four weeks' duration and was similar in lots of ways to my Air Bomber Instructors Course, but very much more specialized and this time our flying was on Wellington aircraft so I was more at home on them than in Blenheims. On leaving Manby after this latest feast of knowledge I felt very confident that I now possessed the necessary qualifications to become a bombing leader on an operational squadron.

On my arrival back at Lichfield I was immediately appointed Assistant Chief Ground Instructor, so felt that the pass obtained on this course had justified my appointment.

It was about this time that I had been giving some serious consideration to volunteering for a tour of duty with Pathfinder Force, the squadrons who marked the targets for the main force bombers. I felt with my tour of operations on Halifaxes behind me and with two specialist courses recently completed I had something to offer this force as a Visual Bomb Aimer Marker. I had always admired the work of PFF and had always a great desire to join their ranks. Before deciding to return to operational flying it was interesting to look at the situation existing in the Middle East and European Theatres of War.

In the Middle East the war in North Africa had ended with the defeat of Rommel and the German Afrika Korps in May 1943. In July 1943 the Allies invaded Sicily and by August 1943 all German resistance in that island had ceased and an Allied landing was made in Southern Italy at the beginning of September. By then Italy had got rid of Mussolini and a few days later surrendered unconditionally to the Allies. But the Germans were not finished in Italy and made a quick military occupation of the country, intending to make the Allies fight for every inch of territory. The German front in Italy was strong and contained many divisions and the fierce fighting that took place in the mountainous terrain made advancing slow and laborious and even with complete air superiority the campaign was not an easy one. The victories that freed Naples and Rome were quite magnificent, but there was quite a way to go before all Italy was free.

On the Russian front the initiative had rested with the Red Army since 1943 when in their summer/autumn offensive they had overthrown the bastions of Bryansk, Orel, Kharkov, Stazino and Taganrog and had made a great drive to the south-east towards the Dnieper. At the end of 1943 the German domination of the Eastern Front was shrinking and in the Balkans the Red Army had forced Rumania and Bulgaria to seek armistice terms. It looked as if the Russians had now got the upper hand.

In Britian Harris had started the Battle of Berlin in August 1943 and this battle was to continue into the early months of 1944 with many large destructive raids on the city. About March 1944 some Bomber Command aircraft were diverted from the mass bombing of cities to smaller targets that would be important to the Germans when the Allies made their invasion attack: targets such as marshalling yards, important to the German communications system. Many yards around Paris in

Northern France and the Low Countries were to be completely destroyed, not forgetting that marshalling yards inside Germany were always receiving attention from our bombers. Other targets such as gun emplacements on the Normandy coast and at Dieppe, radar and W/T Stations at Cherbourg and many other small but important objectives such as airfields, oil supplies, ammunition dumps, all called for the bombers' attention in preparation for the D-Day Landings.

The Second Front opened on 6th June 1944 on the beaches of Normandy. The Allies' aim was to establish a beachhead and the quick capture of a port, Cherbourg. The Allied armies met fierce resistance from the Germans as they stormed the beaches on D-Day and both sides had many casualties. It was fortunate for the Allies that they had complete air supremacy in the area of landing. After getting men and equipment ashore there was still much fighting to be done and it was mid-August before the Battle of Normandy was won and the American forces swept towards Paris into Brittany and the British forces, staying nearer the coast, advanced towards Boulogne and Calais.

Now that the Second Front was opened I was keen to get back on operational flying, so volunteered for PFF at the beginning of August and was posted to the PFF Navigation Training Unit at Warboys on 21st August 1944 for a two week course. During my days at Warboys I carried out some eight air exercises, mainly dropping practice bombs and got the impression if I could achieve good results on the practice bombing range, then I would be on my way to an operational squadron very quickly. As it turned out, my bombing results were all very acceptable and I was posted to No 7 Pathfinder Squadron at RAF Oakington near Cambridge on 28 August 1944. So once again I was back on an operational squadron and, believe it or not, was pleased to be there. I was really looking forward to the challenge of marking targets for the main force bombers.

Oakington was probably the best RAF station I had come across and was in lots of ways similar to RAF Linton-on-Ouse. It was a beautiful airfield with good runways and splendid pre-war buildings. I got the feeling that this was a very fine operational station. I was not be to be disappointed as on arrival at the officers' mess I found it was like a hotel compared to Holme on Spalding Moor or Lichfield. The weather was fine and sunny and I immediately fell in love with this station and all the surrounding countryside, including the city of Cambridge.

CHAPTER VIII

Pathfinder Force

From the beginning of the war to the spring of 1942 it was quite apparent to the Air Staff that some sort of target marking was required to achieve better bombing results on enemy targets. In the early part of the war it was not always easy for crews to navigate accurately on DR Navigation especially when the weather was against them, so it was quite understandable that often aircraft did not reach their targets. Harris had always fought against any move to form an elite marking force. An attempt had been made in the spring of 1942 to light the targets with incendiaries dropped from a lead aircraft and this had met with some success. About the middle of 1942 Harris was being pressed by the Air Staff, especially the ones with operational experience, to form a marker force. Still resisting, he had to yield to pressure and so the Pathfinder Force was formed in August 1942.

Harris picked a young 32-year-old group captain by the name of Donald Bennett, an Australian, to command No 8 Group Pathfinder Force. Bennett had served under Harris on flying boats pre-war and then left the RAF to fly with Imperial Airways. On his return to the RAF in the early part of the war he commanded a Halifax squadron until he was shot down while attacking the *Tirpitz* in a Norwegian Fjord, but made a successful escape through Sweden.

I first met Air Vice Marshal Bennett when he addressed our intake at PFF Navigation Training Unit at Warboys. He struck me then as being a brilliant officer and I was never to change my mind on this all the time I served on PFF. I remember after his

Air Vice Marshal D.C.T. Bennett, CB, CBE, DSO, AFRAeS

talk one officer who had served under Bennett was to tell me that his knowledge of aircrew and aircraft was frightening as he seemed to have greater knowledge and detail of all crew members' jobs then they had. Stories would abound about how he would tie perhaps a navigator, or a wireless operator in knots with his questions when they appeared before him on a commissioning interview. He was such a brilliant man that I do not think he suffered fools gladly, and I think perhaps that made him seem arrogant at times. Harris, describing Bennett to Winston Churchill said, 'One of the most efficient and the finest youngsters I have ever come across in the Service.'

My admiration for Bennett had started long before arriving in 8 Group as I remembered reading his book *The Complete Air Navigator* early on in the war. The book to me at that time contained some of the most up-to-date air navigation that was available and it was invaluable to me when I started RAF training. Only a few years ago at a reunion I was talking with Donald Bennett about his book and he assured me that this had been written on his honeymoon. I do not think that I ever met a more brilliant man all during my 23 years in the Royal Air Force. As Air Officer Commanding 8 Group, he was a great commander and his knowledge of aircrew and aircraft was truly magnificent and gained the respect of all who served in his elite force.

Air Vice Marshal Bennett was ultimately to build up No 8 Group PFF to a total of 19 squadrons and was to devise methods of target marking that were to ensure the success of a very large number of bombing raids. The tour of operations on a Pathfinder squadron was 45 sorties, but in the case of aircrew like myself who had completed a tour on main force bombers our tour would be 20 operations.

Harris and Bennett had managed to secure from Air Ministry some recognition for aircrew on PFF squadrons. The first was a step up in rank and pay while on PFF operational squadrons, but this was to be relinquished at the end of one's tour. Secondly was the award of the coveted Pathfinder Force Badge, awarded on a temporary basis after a few marker operations on the squadron, with the permanent award coming after 20 marker operations. The badge was a gold-coloured metal eagle with wings spread and was worn on the flap of the breast pocket of one's uniform tunic below any decorations and medal ribbons.

On arrival at 7 Squadron I was pleased to find the Lancaster bombers so well equipped with the latest navigation and marking aids. These consisted of GEE and H2S. The Lancaster appealed to me as a very fine bomber and on my few trips at Warboys I admired it very much. The four Rolls–Royce Merlin Engines could carry a bomb load of 14,000 lbs with fuel for 1,660 miles and had a cruising speed of 216 mph with a maximum of 266 mph.

The Gee equipment I knew about as we had carried this on Halifaxes. It was a good accurate method of fixing position, but was dependent on UK ground radio stations and was limited in range, but now our forces were in Europe the range could be increased with European stations. H2S was airborne radar equipment sending out beams and picking up the reflected ground returns on a cathode ray tube in the aircraft. It would give a picture of the ground below, but sometimes was very hazy. Coastlines showed up well as did the shape of towns. This was a great aid when flying above cloud. This H2S equipment on Pathfinder aircraft was operated by a bomb aimer who was called the set operator and was to become most efficient in reading the pictures picked up on the cathode ray tube and myself as a visual marker bomb aimer was to rely heavily on him for a decent run on the aiming point.

There was one more very effective blind bombing aid and that was Oboe and was a development in methods the Germans had used in bombing the United Kingdom in 1940. The aircraft would fly at the end of a radio beam transmitted by a UK ground station and would drop its markers when reaching the intersection with another beam from a second ground station. The device was carried on Mosquito aircraft flying about 28,000 feet and marking was usually accurate to within a few hundred yards.

The De Havilland Mosquito was ideal for this type of

Lancasters of 156 Squadron, PFF, dropping 'Christmas Trees' (German name for marker flares) from 12,000 feet; Hanau, 18/19th March 1945.

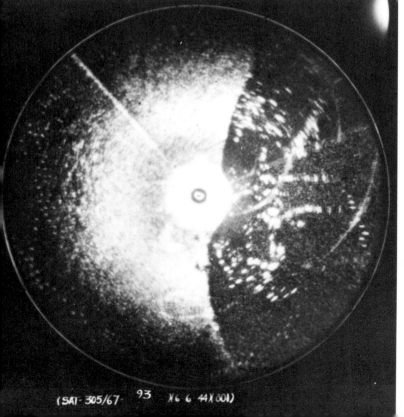

H2S photo of the Normandy invasion fleet.

(SAT-305/67 93 X6 6 44X 001)

operation. It flew quite high, had a speed of 350 mph, was most manoeuverable and therefore was no easy target for German fighter aircraft. PFF had been given some priority in the delivery of Mosquito aircraft so it was not surprising that by the time I arrived at Oakington there were a few Mosquito squadrons in 8 Group.

By September 1944 Pathfinder squadrons had quite a number of sophisticated techniques for target marking which had all been tried and tested and proved most effective. The selection of a particular type of marking for a raid was purely dependent upon the weather conditions that would exist at the target area during the attack. The main techniques were code-named Wanganui, Paramatta (Musical and Oboe), and Newhaven.

Wanganui was probably the least effective of all the marking methods and was only used when the target area and aiming point was completely covered by cloud and the bombers had no chance of seeing any ground detail. By navigating the Wanganui marking aircraft by H2S to the target area and by dropping sky markers on top of the cloud, the bomber stream would then drop their bombs through the markers and the cloud on to the target below. With the drift of the target indicators sometimes in quite high winds, it was not surprising that bombs could be spread over a wide area. This method was used only when other methods were impossible.

Paramatta (Musical and Oboe) ground marking was by blind dropped ground markers, Newhaven target marking was blind by H2S supported by visual backers-up.

It was necessary on a primary visual attack that the weather was good enough to see the ground. Perhaps in the target area the attack would open with a Mosquito dropping a marker by Oboe. This was always very comforting for the Lancasters approaching the target as the set operators were guiding them towards their aiming point. The primary visual marker aircraft had the visual bomb aimer who would ultimately identify the target and mark it with probably red target indicators. Just ahead of the primary visual marker were the blind illuminators, about ten aircraft carrying parachute flares and they would illuminate the target so that the primary visual marker bomb aimer could map read his way onto the target. When he could see and identify the aiming point he would aim his markers with his MK XIV bombsight and hope like hell it hit the right spot because the first wave of bombers would be bombing almost immediately, and probably several hundreds, a few minutes later. This initial marker would be backed up by other target indicators from PFF aircraft at the head of each wave of bombers, so the aiming point would be kept marked for the full duration of the raid.

A variation of this was the Master Bomber controlled attack where two aircraft controlled the whole attack; one with the Master Bomber and the other with Deputy Master Bomber. This type of attack perhaps out of Oboe range would open by the blind illuminating aircraft dropping their flares just ahead of the Master and Deputy and the eight or so supporting aircraft around them. These supporting aircraft were carrying bombs and not markers and their primary function was to help protect the Master and Deputy by distracting some of the defences. As the target came into view of the visual bomb aimer, probably in the Deputy Master's aircraft, he would know what ground detail to note on the run up to aiming point, then if he could positively identify the spot he would drop his target indicators, usually red, by means of his bombsight. Immediately they hit the ground the Master would assess it and give directions to the main force bombers by R/T as to how they should drop their bombs. Sometimes it was:

'Bomb the Red TIs.'

'Overshoot the Red TIs by one second.'

'Bomb one TI width to the starboard of the Red TIs.'

and sure enough there was the first wave bombs hitting at the target. The Deputy Master would climb away to orbit above the bombers keeping the target in view while the Master would make another run to put down more red indicators on the aiming point and then climbing away to get above the incoming bombers and orbit the target giving instructions to the next waves coming in and telling the PFF backers up, probably one or

Airborne: a Lancaster leaves base en route to the Ruhr

Munster 'all lit up'

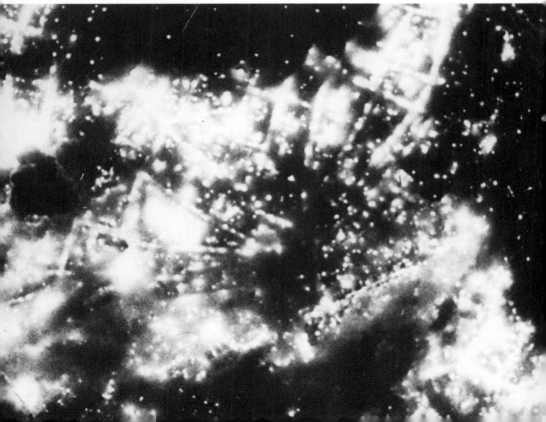

two at the head of each wave, where to drop their green target indicators. The supporters meantime would have made a second run with their bomb doors open and got rid of their bomb load on the markers. Master and Deputy would keep orbiting keeping the target in view and the Master ensuring the correct area was being hit by his precise instructions to the main force bombers. Only when the last wave had gone through the target was it time for the Master and Deputy to leave.

On occasions when it was intended to use ground marking, on arrival at the target it was found that due to cloud it was impossible to place markers on the aiming point so that they could be seen by the main force bombers then. The Master Bomber would call for a Wanganui attack and sky markers would be used so that the raid would not have to be aborted.

From my explanations on different types of marking you will realize that crews each had a particular role to play. Some roles called for crews to carry bombs and others to carry target indicators and the roles were allocated according to the experience of the crews. The new and inexperienced crews on first joining the squadron would be given the supporter aircraft role. This would mean, say, in the Master Bomber type attack, six or eight aircraft would accompany the Master and Deputy aircraft into the target area to ensure defences would not be concentrating on only two aircraft. These supporter aircraft would be carrying bombs and would make a second run on the target to drop them on the markers put down by the Master or Deputy.

Crews with a little more experience would be given the blind illuminating role and would drop flares so that the aiming point could be identified and marked by the Master and Deputy. Experienced crews carrying target indicators would be employed on the visual backer-up role where perhaps one or two aircraft at the head of each wave of bombers would drop target indicators as directed by the R/T messages from the Master Bomber. Certain crews would carry sky marking indicators and would drop if ordered to do so by the Master Bomber.

The most experienced crews would be given the Master or

Deputy Master role or the primary visual marker role in that type of attack. The Master or Deputy was not an easy role and one of the most hazardous of all types of attack as it often meant spending 15 to 20 minutes or more in the target area directing the attack and it was not unusual for these aircraft to be hit several times. One had to carry a great amount of good luck to survive as a Master or Deputy.

CHAPTER IX

7 Squadron Oakington

In my first few days at Oakington I spent my time finding my way around the various sections on the station, meeting people and getting to know the layout of the airfield. I was introduced to the crew I would be flying with on my first few operations. My captain was Flying Officer Protheroe and he and his crew were a very friendly lot and made me most welcome as their visual marker bomb aimer.

The whole crew were quite experienced in the supporter and illuminating roles and were just reaching the stage when they would be carrying target indicators. They were being promoted to the visual backers-up role, hence the reason for my joining the crew as a visual bomb aimer marker. I obviously would have to do quite a number of visual backer-up raids to gain experience in marking before being given a chance to prove myself as a primary visual marker. On our first few days together a practice bombing flight and a cross-country exercise let us get in some practice working as a crew. On 11th September 1944 I was to carry out my first raid as a visual backer-up marker on a target called Kamen in the Ruhr. This was a daylight raid and was quite short, only lasting about 3 hours 45 minutes and proved quite successful. Our job was to back up the markers already on the ground and by the time we appeared over the target, probably at the head of the second or third wave of bombers, the raid was going well with high explosive bombs bursting all around the target indicators. There appeared to be dying red target indicators and some green still burning brightly so as instructed I dropped my green target indicators on to the ones on the ground. They fell quite close, so I was satisfied with my first marking operation. The flak was of medium intensity and we managed to negotiate it without much trouble. I felt from what I had seen in daylight that evening of the Ruhr defences, that they were not nearly so ferocious as the barrage I had encountered on my night raids in 1943. Perhaps the fact it was daylight made it appear less frightening.

On 12th September another daylight raid saw us pay a visit to the city of Munster and on the 13th yet another daylight raid to the Ruhr town of Gelsenkirchen-Nordstern where we were to experience some extremely heavy flak, so the Ruhr had not yet capitulated and was still a very dangerous area.

On the 17th in daylight we were ordered to Boulogne to attack German gun emplacements in support of the advancing British Army and then again in daylight on the 20th we went to attack the German garrison at Calais. These were quite straightforward raids and we encountered no flak as we dropped our target indicators to back up the ones on the ground. I was always extremely pleased to see my markers go down in the right place when we were engaged in support of the Army, as on occasions where our own troops were not too far away from our objective it would only need a small error to find markers landing amongst advancing Allied troops. This would have been disastrous as bombs would follow unless the Master Bomber was quick enough to cancel the misplaced markers with a white smoke marker and also warn the incoming bombers by an R/T message.

I never seemed to escape from the Ruhr targets for any great length of time, so it was back there to Neuss on the night of the 23rd, when our main attack was concentrated on the railway yards. I found the flak barrage very concentrated as shells seemed to be bursting all round the aircraft as we tracked in to place our TIs on the aiming point. I was quite pleased to get out of this area around Düsseldorf as to me it had always been a very active heavy flak area. After this raid I was to appreciate even more that there was still a lot of fight left in the Germans and there appeared to be no shortage of anti-aircraft shells.

An attack on the German garrison at Calais on the 25th had to be aborted due to the aiming point being completely enveloped in heavy cloud, but the Germans were not so lucky on the morning of 27th September when a full scale attack bombed the garrison and in my mind it was a great success, as we were never to return to this channel port and shortly after this raid the Allied armies in the area were to continue their advance.

These tactical raids in support of the Allied ground troops were paying dividends and proved that the strategic bombers could be used very successfully in this close support tactical role. This meant that when the Army advance was being slowed or halted by enemy action, a call could be made for bomber support. On this last raid to Calais I had operated with another crew captained by Flying Officer Ken Rawson, an Australian. His whole crew impressed me very much as being a keen, well drilled, well disciplined outfit. His crew members were: navigator Jack Willie, set operator Sid Rorrison, wireless operator Bernie Elsworthy, flight engineer Sam Bowman, mid-upper gunner Jock Stewart, and rear gunner Alan Camlin. This crew had recently been promoted to the visual backer-up role and I was pleased to join them as their visual marker bomb aimer.

I hoped that with a skipper as keen as Ken Rawson and with such an efficient crew we could perhaps one day become a primary visual marker or even a Master Bomber crew. I had a long chat with Ken when joining his crew and we both appeared to be ambitious about being employed in the Master Bomber role and from what I had seen of the high navigation standard of Jack Willie, the H2S set operating of Sid Rorrison and the efficiency of the others I only hoped I could fit into the crew and we could all prove by our results that we were the material required for the Master Bomber role. I felt we had the potential and all we required was to be given the opportunity to prove ourselves.

The city of Duisburg was to come in for some severe punishment from Bomber Command on 14th October when we took off at 07.09 for a daylight attack which was to consist of an attack by about 1,000 bombers and then at 23.15 hours that

126

Avro Lancaster Mk I in flight.

Calais on the 25th September 1944 viewed from 6,500 feet.

night we took off to attack the city once again with about a thousand bombers taking part. Both attacks seemed to go well, but as usual the defences were very active. On the daylight raid bombs could be seen crashing into the buildings and large and small explosions seemed to be everywhere as thick black smoke, probably from oil tank fires, was drifting across the city. One wondered just how much could have been left standing after the night raid following this devastating daylight attack. Those two raids with my new crew proved to me that they were a good crew and I was pleased I had joined them.

Having returned from Duisberg about 03.40, after debriefing we had managed about six hours' sleep before finding that once again we were on our way to Germany, this time to the northern port of Wilhelmshaven. We took off at 17.20 hours so things were really hectic and Harris was not giving his crews much sleeping time. We arrived over the target to find a moderate flak barrage with the usual number of searchlights waving around. We seemed to be into the target very quickly, dropped our markers and were out without having to take much evasive action. There may have been a few fighters around, but they were not to bother us as navigator Jack Willie passed the new course to Ken; our nose was pointed towards England and our four engines were churning through the night air. I liked these targets where one could escape fairly quickly from ground defences to the relative safety of being above the North Sea.

Operating at this stage of the war even on a PFF squadron I was not feeling the pressure that I had experienced in Halifaxes in 1943 during the Battles of the Ruhr and Hamburg. Perhaps the fact that in June 1943 in nearly 6,000 night sorties, 275 aircraft were missing and in September 1944, for about 6,500 night and nearly 10,000 day sorties the loss was 140 aircraft from a total of 16,500. From these figures one need not be a mathematician to realize that operational aircrew now had a much greater chance of survival.

Now that Thousand Bomber Raids were commonplace and target marking by PFF had been perfected, results were being achieved that hitherto would have been unthinkable. Daylight

Squadron Leader Ken Rawson and crew beside a 7 Squadron PFF Lancaster in early 1945. *(Rear)* Ken Rawson with *(in front)* Bernie Elsworthy. *(Front, left to right)* The author, Jock Stewart, Alan Camlin, Jack Willie, Sam Bowman, Sid Rorrison.

HQ PFF Ops Room board for the night of Saturday, 14th October 1944. Targets: Duisburg, Berlin, Ludwigshaven, Hamburg and Düsseldorf. A typical routing plan with markers, bombers, spoofs etc.

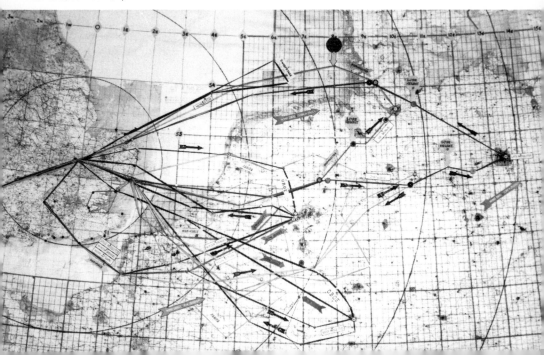

and night bombing could be carried out at will with little or no interference from the German fighter aircraft, but the ground defences in the Ruhr and other big cities still appeared to be well manned and extremely active and at no time were they to be underestimated.

Most operational crews felt at this time that probably we were in the home stretch and victory was possible in the next few months, provided the Allied advance in Europe could be maintained and the Russians could keep up their winning way on the Eastern Front.

I was settling down well with my new crew and I liked the people on 7 Squadron and although Harris was keeping us busy, I found some keen golfers and we would escape to Gog Me Gog at Cambridge for a quick round and a few jugs of beer at the Nineteenth. What a wonderful way golfing had of making one forget about operational flying. Any other spare time would be spent careering around the Cambridgeshire countryside on the pillion of Rawson's motorbike or visiting the rather nice pubs like the Baron of Beef in the city of Cambridge. I fell in love with the great city and never missed an opportunity to visit its many colleges and places of interest.

Harris was to continue with his relentless area bombing of the German cities and the end of October was to see Stuttgart on the 19th, Essen on the 23rd and again on the 25th visited by our crew. On the last daylight attack on Essen it was difficult to see just exactly what was being achieved. I can only guess that factories or workshops were still in production somewhere in this city that appeared to have been razed to the ground with very few buildings standing. There were buildings with the inside burned out and only a few walls left standing; there were piles of rubble everywhere and I wondered what they did about water, food and electricity. These problems must have been enormous. I wondered if any of their factories were still producing and was to get a reminder they were, as a host of Ack-Ack shells burst all around us.

I knew the Germans to be very resilient in the past in repairing and rebuilding their plants and railways, but I now felt that time was running out for them and with the Allied armies on their doorstep they were facing certain defeat.

Bomber Command had now reached its zenith as Harris could muster about 1,600 bombers for day and night bombing. He had fought a long time to build up this huge force and I had the distinct impression that he would make good use of it to ensure that the war was brought to a successful conclusion at the earliest possible moment. He was to continue his area bombing with a small percentage of his force being used for oil, fuel and communications targets. Army support operations were carried out when requested by the Army.

Harris had perhaps failed to achieve his objective of forcing the surrender of the Germans by area bombardment, but I feel fairly sure had he commanded such a large number of bombers two years earlier and had the expertise of Pathfinder Force that he now possessed, then there was a fair chance his objective may have been achieved with the help of the US Eighth Air Force.

After seventeen sorties in which the crew had carried markers and had been employed in the visual backer-up role, it was time for us to be rated good enough for the primary visual marker role and were given this role on 9th November 1944 when we were ordered to mark the synthetic oil plant at Wanne Eickel in the Ruhr. I was extremely pleased for myself and the crew that we had reached this standard as Ken Rawson, the Skipper, and all the others, were very keen. It will be remembered that the crew consisted of eight in the visual marking roles, the categories being, one pilot, a navigator responsible for the chart work, bomb aimer, responsible for operation of the H2S (set operator), wireless operator responsible for W/T signals, two air gunners (one in the mid-upper gun turret and one in the rear turret), the flight engineer and myself as visual bomb aimer marker.

A great amount of the success of a raid of this sort depended just how well I could identify the aiming point and mark it accurately with my target indicators because the main force bombers would be aiming at this target indicator only a couple of minutes or so after it was on the ground and they did not expect Pathfinders to make mistakes. I would be guided into the

(*Left*) Group Captain T.G. — 'Hamish' — Mahaddie, DSO, DFC, AFC, the man chiefly responsible for selecting suitable crews for operations with the PFF (No 8 Group).

(*Below*) PFF HQ Ops Room meeting. From the left: W/Cdr Benny Finn (Senior OBOE controller); John Jukes; Tommy (Met), AVM Don Bennett; SASO (obscured here), Rathbone (Armt). Duty Naval Officer in background, and unidentified officer nearest with back to camera.

target area by the set operator from his picture on H2S until such a time as I could identify my position and guide our aircraft on to the aiming point. Prior to take-off it was very necessary that the visual marker crew, especially pilot and bomb aimer, studied all the available target maps and any available photographs of the target and also what ground detail to expect on the run in on the aiming point. Ken and myself spent a considerable time acquainting ourselves with as much detail as we could absorb. Fortunately, being a daylight trip it would be easier to recognize ground detail.

We took off at 08.30 and arrived in the target area about 10.30 hours to find the whole area in cloud cover and impossible for any visual marking, so sky marking was necessary. I was very disappointed; however, I hoped it would not be too long before we would be given another opportunity.

A couple of days later we were back to Dortmund for a night raid and I remembered this was where it had all started for me on Halifaxes in May 1943. A lot had happened since then and I only wished this had been a daylight attack to allow me to see just how much of this city remained standing. The sortie on this occasion, I think, was a little less hazardous than back in 1943. At least I wrote in my log book that the flak was moderate. I felt at this time that the continuing onslaught on the Ruhr by the large numbers of aircraft available for each raid must in the end cause the collapse of the German economy.

On 16th November 1944 the position of the Allied armies as winter was settling upon the Continent was that the British had advanced to the forest and woodlands of the Ardennes and slightly to the south, the Americans were pushing through Luxembourg towards the Saar Palatinate and were not too far from the Moselle and in the distance were the cities of the Ruhr. So poised on these lines and with lots of hard campaigning ahead of them it was not surprising that Bomber Command were doing all in their power to smooth the armies' passage into Germany.

The communications along the west side of the Rhine were the ones that the Wehrmacht would depend on when opposing the Allied armies, so many of these were to receive the attention of

Harris during a period about mid-November and on the 16th we were ordered to Jülich, a place I had never heard of before, but from the map found it was on the Roer River and I would have thought of it as a quiet town. However, it must have been quite an important part of the overall German communication system, so was to receive quite a hefty raid to ensure rail and road traffic would not move smoothly for some time to come. The raid from the crew's point of view was quite successful, as having found the defences to be moderate in intensity we escaped without harm.

At the end of November the crew were granted a week's well-earned leave and I was to take Ken to Scotland to visit my folks and show him a bit of our fine Scottish scenery. Arriving back at Oakingtin feeling refreshed after our holiday in the north it was straight into action with the night raids to Karlsruhe, Osnabrück, Essen and Duisburg on the 4th, 6th, 12th and 17th of December respectively, so Harris was making sure that his bomber force would never be left idle and that no German city would be safe from his bombers so long as Hitler continued to wage war.

Essen still seemed to have strong defences, but nothing like what they had been in 1943. In no way was the C-in-C going to allow a city like Essen to produce any weapons or any other war materials if he could possibly stop them, so my guess was that he had already gone a long way towards his objective and very little production was being achieved in this once great industrial city, and I felt quite certain this could be said for many of the other German cities at this time.

During this period of the war it was sometimes difficult to see what was left to bomb in the already bombed-out cities, but if Sir Arthur Harris and his intelligence service felt that some place needed the attention of the bombers, then this was good enough for his aircrews. The Commander-in-Chief had such a large number of bombers and aircrews available that places that had not been bombed previously were now in line for his attention. Many raids were now being carried out on oil and communications targets, although I never thought Harris strayed far from his overall desire of area bombing of the German cities.

I had hoped that perhaps this war would have been over by Christmas 1944, but as the festive season drew nearer it became more and more clear that the Germans still intended fighting to the bitter end in the defence of their homeland and somehow or other they did not appear on the surface to be short of weapons for their front line troops. It was known from intelligence services that their fuel supplies were low and this appeared their biggest drawback along with lack of manpower in their fighting services. The USAAF aided by Bomber Command must be given full credit for their efforts in bringing the German oil industry to the point of collapse. About the middle of December weather conditions on the Continent had deteriorated and snow had fallen in and around the area of the Ardennes where the British Army lines were a bit stretched and the cold miserable conditions were not making campaigning easy.

It was in these conditions that Von Rundstedt mounted an attack on 16th December on a broad front from Monschau in the north to Echtranach in the south. Panzers moved fast through the snow-covered wooded countryside and German armoured units cut into the American lines. The advance was so rapid that many forward positions were overrun and troops were fighting for their lives as Tiger tanks roared in making a path for advancing infantry. Von Rundstedt with no air support and precious little fuel was hoping for a quick success while the low clouds and fog kept Allied Tempest and Mustang aircraft grounded.

The aim of the German attack was to drive towards Antwerp and separate the two major Allied army groups and for a few days the weather was on the Germans' side, but Allied resistance was strengthened and on the 24th the 29th British Armoured Brigade halted the Panzers near Dinant.

On the 24th, Christmas Eve, the weather all over England was fog and the visibility at Oakington was not more than about 200 yards. We had been briefed for a daylight attack on Mulheim-Essen airport with take-off at 12.00 hours and had

Seeing 'em off: Erks (ground crew) wave a final good luck to a Lanc crew as the Lanc gathers momentum on its take-off run.

Fire-load. SBCs of incendiaries awaiting loading into a Lanc.

been warned that in all probability if the fog was still persisting on our return, we would receive a diversion to a fog free airfield or to one using FIDO. I was not looking forward to a diversion away from Oakington on Christmas Eve, then I thought of our soldiers probably cold and miserable in the forests of the Ardennes and thought how lucky we were to be stationed in the United Kingdom.

The fog still persisted as we took off at noon with visibility no better but having climbed a few hundred feet we were in brilliant sunshine above the cloud layer. The cloud layer over the Continent was extensive and we were not to get a break in it till quite near the target area when we could see ground detail and identify the airfield. The markers were dropped accurately and the main force were soon crashing their bombs on to the airfield even although the flak was quite intense at times.

I was pleased that we had managed to bomb this place out of action because no doubt this would be a back-up airfield for the enemy's Ardennes Offensive.

On the way back across the North Sea the crew kept hoping that we may be able to land at Oakington but it was not to be and we were diverted to Woodbridge, a very large emergency airfield near Ipswich. On landing at Woodbridge it looked as if half of the Bomber Command Aircraft had arrived here and also some USAAF aircraft. We were to find just how crowded the station was when we arrived at the very small officers' mess where the only place I found to sit down was in a corridor and to make things worse the weather outside was bitterly cold.

As the fog was not clearing we had to spend the night in this very small mess and I had to try and sleep on the ante-room floor in my flying kit after having downed a few beers to ease the agony.

Next day, Christmas Day, there was no let up in the fog, so our AOC, Air Vice Marshal Bennett, had ordered coaches from Oakington to pick up the crews and return them to Oakington so that we could get a decent night's sleep. After quite a hair-raising journey by coach through the fogbound countryside we arrived early afternoon at Oakington and I have never known a bath to be so relaxing.

That night we had a Christmas dinner of sorts and there was an officers' mess dance which was most enjoyable. After several drinks it was wonderful to forget that perhaps tomorrow you would be once again dicing with death over the Valley of the Ruhr. On climbing into my bed that night I did not need any rocking as I had some sleep to catch up on.

After an enforced holiday on Boxing Day due to weather conditions the squadron aircrew were rudely awakened at 04.00 hours on the 27th and after an early breakfast were on our way by coach to Woodbridge to collect the aircraft we had left there on Christmas Eve. The weather conditions were improving and we managed to get airborne at Woodbridge about midday and in 35 minutes were back at Oakington.

I fully expected with all this urgency to get the aircraft back to base that we would be scheduled for operations that night as the German offensive in the Ardennes was still being treated with some concern. I was wrong as the weather conditions on the Continent were still pretty foul, so it was not until the afternoon of the 30th that we were briefed for a raid on marshalling yards at Cologne and at this briefing we were to find that the Allies now had the whip-hand in the Ardennes and their advnace was continuing.

I was not surprised that Cologne was being attacked, especially the marshalling yards, as any communications in this area were critical for the German forces opposing the Allied advance towards the Moselle and the cities of the Ruhr. This was my fourth visit to Cologne, and I wondered if the twin spires of the Cathedral were still standing. I had been to the Ruhr so many times now I knew the geography of the place like the back of my hand, but was never to know any way in or out of the place without running into the ever active defences. These defences never ceased to keep me on edge as I had seen far too many of our aircraft being shot from the sky in this area. It was the same old story, one diving down out of control and others being blown up in one huge flash. It was sights like these that made me feel the pit of my stomach as I breathed heavily in my oxygen mask and watched to see how many parachutes if any came from the doomed aircraft.

On this occasion the searchlights were there, but not in such large numbers and the flak seemed a bit subdued from my previous visits but still there was enough for my liking and off to port I saw a huge flash in the sky and hated to think that another of our aircraft had bitten the dust.

It was just after 20.30 hours when we made our bombing run and dropped our markers. Looking at the ground as my markers exploded near the aiming point it was from the light of the flares I thought I could see the twin spires of the Cathedral still standing. I was just thinking it was not all good bomb aiming that managed to miss those Cathedral spires; I felt that some other power might have had a say in it. Just then it was time to do some more weaving as shrapnel rattled the under belly of our fuselage as we continued through the target and the navigator passed the westerly course for home. I thought thank goodness, not far to go before we would be over our own army lines and away from the flak. Looking back on leaving the target area, I felt there was a dying city and I did not think I would need to visit it for a fifth time. Perhaps it would be a relief for the citizens when our armies arrived and the bombing would cease.

We arrived safely at Oakington at 23.00 and with only 31st December to come I hoped we had finished for 1944. We were not required to operate on the 31st, so like a true Scot I managed to get invited to a good Hogmanay Party in Cambridge and must have tried awfully hard to drink myself under the table. I was distinctly fragile when I awoke on 1st January and Rawson, my Skipper, was telling me to get out of bed – we were going on operations. It was not till I had leaped out of bed and was shaving that he informed me that we had the day off, so my language to him was quite choice. In a way I was quite pleased he had got me out of bed as I wanted to arrange a golf match for that afternoon as fresh air would do me a power of good, so after lunch it was off to the Gog Me Gog course.

At the beginning of 1945 the British nation had been at war for

139

five years and four months and I am sure they all felt as I did that they were on the threshold of a great victory and it was only a major setback that would prolong the war. Setbacks or hiccups, like Arnhem and the Ardennes, were now behind our advancing Allied armies and the advance was headed towards the German homeland as the occupied countries were being liberated and the German Army was in retreat. On the eastern front the Russians were continuing their advance but the Germans seemed to put up tremendous resistance in certain areas and casualties on both sides were heavy. The Allies had made it clear to the Germans that the only surrender they would accept would be unconditional, so this was not to be easily accepted by the Third Reich, so the fighting was to continue even although in this phase of the war the bomber force had done much to bring the German economy to its knees. German oil supplies were now at a critically low level and the continuing attacks on rail, water and road communications were bleeding German industry to death.

At this point in the war if Hitler had been a reasonable man he would have surrendered to save the lives of many of his troops, but he was not a reasonable man and the war was to continue.

So long as Germany continued fighting, Harris, with a bigger bomber force than ever, would ensure they were not left idle, so it was on 2nd January 1945 that we were briefed as primary visual marker crew for Nuremberg. I was quite pleased to be given the primary marker's job, so I hoped I would get a good view of the target as I studied the photographs and target map. Nuremberg was not the type of target that had been kind to RAF aircrew in the past, as Bomber Command had lost many aircraft on previous raids.

The afternoon take-off was at 15.50 and we were over the target about 19.05 hours and after a very good run into the city on H2S I was able to pick up the aiming point and mark the target visually. The whole raid seemed to be striking home on the city and bombs appeared to be exploding around the markers so I assumed I could count this a successful attack as 520 bombers were involved and seemed to be hitting the city

Avro Lancaster on daylight sortie

where it counted most. The defences were quite active in the city area and I would guess the flak barrage was intense in places. There were plenty of shells exploding around us and some were a bit close for comfort as some shrapnel could be heard rattling the fuselage, so it was:

'Keep weaving, Skipper,'

and we were soon breathing a sigh of relief as we cleared the main defences and turned on to a westerly course. The journey home was to take about three and a half hours and although the fighters may have been fewer in numbers, vigilance was still necessary to ensure against the surprise attacks. We ran the gauntlet and had quite an uneventful return flight arriving back at base at 23.00 hours. At debriefing the returning crews all thought the raid was successful, so I was pleased they agreed with me.

Two nights later I was primary visual marker on Hanover but cloud completely obscured the target and sky marking was necessary. I was very disappointed but with cloud amounts of this sort visual marking was impossible. Similar conditions again existed at Hanau on the 6th and a Wanganui attack took place. On the 7th it was another night raid, to Munich. A Munich trip to me always meant quite a long time over enemy territory as the round trip was likely to last about 7 hours. The weatherman had forecast good weather enroute, but was forecasting large amounts of cloud in the Munich area, so it was odds on that it would be a Wanganui attack; the chances were, however, that as about 650 bombers were on the raid that if the sky marking was accurate, many bombs would fall on the city.

By the time we were nearing the target we were above a complete blanket of cloud, so it was not long before the sky markers were being dropped on top of the cloud and the bombers were attacking through the markers and the bombs were crashing down on the city. As the anti-aircraft shells started bursting around us I was quite surprised how many bombers I could see all round, as they seemed to be reflected against the cloud below us. One Lancaster I could see quite near us and as I kept an eye on him there appeared to be a large flash from his

142

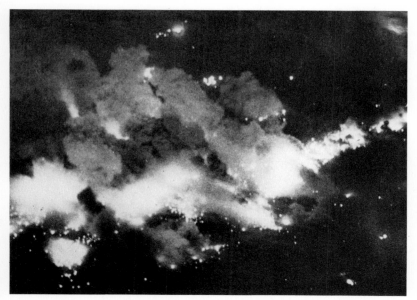

Munich night scene on 21st December 1944

aircraft as he started down into the cloud layer. But for me it was:

'Keep weaving, Skipper,'

as with nose down we headed through the target area. As I looked down at the cloud layer several thousand feet below, our level of 16,000 feet, there appeared to be explosions lighting up the clouds and I could only guess that some light flak was falling short of our height and exploding around the cloud layer and there was quite a chance that cones of searchlights would be moving about with their beams hitting the underside of the clouds. All this was giving reflected light upwards showing up the bombers. I did not see any night fighters in the area or on the homeward route, so it was plain sailing, arriving over Oakington just after 02.00.

The weather conditions between 7th and 13th January were extremely poor for operational flying, so we had an enforced stand down and were not to resume operations till a raid to

143

Dulmen in the northern part of the Ruhr on the 14th. The weather conditions in the target area turned out to be clear and a very successful raid was carried out on a town which must have been quite important to the Wehrmacht, as a supply base and a centre of communications for troops opposing the advancing Allied armies.

CHAPTER X

Operational Sorties 1945

By the end of January 1945 I was now well into my third tour of operations but in no way had I any intention of leaving 7 Squadron till the end of the European war. Ken Rawson had not completed his tour and I had promised him I would remain with the crew till they finished and, anyway, we still had not made the Master Bomber role which both of us were very keen to achieve. The squadron commander was very pleased I wanted to continue and assured me that it would not be too long before I could expect to carry out a Master Bomber attack.

The position facing the crews on Bomber Command at the beginning of February 1945 was that on raids we had virtually very little fighter aircraft opposition by the Luftwaffe and flak barrages in the big cities were very much subdued, but were still active. The United States Eighth Air Force had done a magnificent job in 1944 by destroying 3,700 German aircraft in their daylight attacks on Germany. The Luftwaffe had lost 44,000 airmen since January 1941, but 13,000 of these had been lost between June and October 1944. These were tremendous losses and it is difficult to imagine any air force standing losses of this magnitude. Added to the Luftwaffe's troubles were the loss of their early warning systems as the Allies advanced in Europe, also their signal communications were being jammed at regular or irregular intervals. No doubt their greatest worry was the very severe shortage of fuel and great credit must be given to the USAAF for their major part in the destruction of the German oil targets, not forgetting the part played by Bomber Command when Harris diverted them from area bombing of cities.

Harris with 1,500 bombers available for operations each day was still mounting raids of 500, 600 and 700 aircraft. With the German defences against our attack now at a very low ebb it was not surprising that the overall losses in Bomber Command dropped to 1% although it would be quite wrong to think that this was so on each target. Often the losses on a particular target could be 3, 4 or 5% so things were not perhaps as easy as they looked – as I was to discover.

Many raids were to be carried out in support of the British and American armies in their advance to the German borders in the west. These raids were usually against communications or garrisons ahead of the advance and would be carried out at 5,000 or 6,000 feet to ensure accuracy. Many raids were carried out in Eastern Germany to places like Leipzig, Chemnitz and others that were in the direct line of advance of the Red Army and were garrison and supply towns for the Wehrmacht.

Although, like myself, most aircrew thought at this stage the war was nearly over, they were quite well aware that the cities of the Ruhr could still put up quite a barrage of flak and that stuff could be lethal. With Harris's obsession for area bombing of towns and cities I was certain that we would be continuing our milk run right to the final whistle.

On the morning of 13th February I was in the crew room when the Bombing Leader informed me that the flight commander wanted a word with me so I made my way to his office.

To my surprise he told me that our crew would not be involved on operations that night but he wanted me to fly on operations with Flight Lieutenant Phillips who was one of the most experienced pilots on the squadron and he and his crew were nearing the end of their tour. It transpired that the squadron commander had promised Phillips that he and his crew would have the opportunity of carrying out a raid as Master Bomber or Deputy before the end of their tour. On this occasion Phillips was to be Deputy Master and I was asked to be his visual marker so I agreed, but I must say I would rather that my own Skipper, Ken Rawson, had been given the Deputy

Master role. However, I suppose he would be given an opportunity at a later date. Ken was a bit annoyed at this situation but we discussed it at some length and came to the conclusion that we did not really mind as we both liked Phillips and his crew. I remember Ken saying,

'Don't you go and get yourself shot down. We still have some Master Bomber trips to do.'

Before the briefing at 16.00 hours I had been to the intelligence office and had spent some time studying photographs and target maps of the target area. The target was the synthetic oil works at Bohlen near Leipzig, so I studied hard all the information we had to hand about the target and noted any pinpoints I should be able to identify on our run in towards the aiming point. As Deputy Master Bomb Aimer I would be first to mark so that the Master would be able to assess just exactly where my markers had landed and give instructions by R/T to the Main Force bombers as to where to bomb in relation to the target indicators.

At briefing I met the rest of the Phillips crew and they immediately impressed me and looked every inch experienced operators and all appeared to be looking forward to their Deputy Master Bomber trip.

The Met Man gave his weather forecast which appeared quite good enroute, but warned us that the weather was very cold in the Leipzig area and we could also expect a fair amount of broken cloud around Bohlen but he did not think that we would have any difficulty seeing our aiming point through the cloud gaps. I discussed the run up to the target with the captain, navigator and H2S operator and we all seemed to be on the same wavelength. After marking we would be climbing above the target and orbiting the target along with the Master aircraft so that we could observe each wave of bombers as they went through the target area and the Master could keep the main force bombers informed on R/T of which markers to take aim at using their bombsights.

We took off from Oakington at 18.40 hours and had quite an uneventful trip enroute to the target area where we found some quite heavy cloud of the cumulus type, but there seemed to be large gaps and as I looked down thought I would be able to see ground detail. A few minutes from the target I could see the blind illuminating aircraft getting rid of their flares which were floating down and I hoped would allow me to see the built-up area and the aiming point. Just ahead of us as the H2S operator guided us into the target area there was a huge gap in the cloud cover and I was beginning to pick up ground detail. I called for bomb doors open as I picked up the aiming point and gave my:

'Left, Left,'

'Steady,'

'Right, Steady,'

instructions to bring the target down my bombsight reflector plate towards release point. As it reached the release point I pressed hard on the bomb release button and watched my target indicators fall from the bomb bay and called for bomb doors closed. The Skipper acknowledged:

'Bomb doors closed,'

I was still looking for our target indicators cascading over the aiming point when all hell seemed to be let loose as there was a very large flash and a God Almighty crash and bang as the shrapnel from the anti-aircraft shells tore into our aircraft. I knew we had been hit and hit badly and as the aircraft shuddered and started losing height, my heart seemed to stand still as I breathed hard into my oxygen mask. The starboard outer engine was on fire and I was getting a terrible cold draught in the bomb aimer's compartment, so I felt sure there must be many holes in the nose area. By the time I had grabbed my parachute and hooked it on my parachute harness I realized that the main damage had occurred on the underside of the fuselage behind the pilot and had penetrated the set operator's position and had badly wounded our set operator.

Another glance to the starboard outer engine showed the Captain had feathered the propeller and managed to extinguish the fire with the engine fire extinguisher. I thanked God for that as I so hated fires in aircraft. We were still losing height and I fully expected to get the 'Abandon Aircraft' order but the

Skipper was doing a magnificent job struggling with the aircraft to try and get us straight and level and keep the aircraft in the air. We had now lost height from 17,000 feet and were down to about 7,000 feet when all of a sudden the captain seemed to succeed in halting our descent and get the aircraft back on a near straight and level course. It looked as if some great hand had reached out and saved us falling out of the sky and I heaved a sigh of relief and breathed hard at my oxygen. The wireless operator was attending our set operator who had a nasty wound on his leg and had lost a lot of blood. He was bandaged up with wound dressings and made as comfortable as possible.

The captain had called the Master Bomber aircraft and warned him we would be leaving the target area due to our unserviceability. We turned on to a westerly course as the navigator passed a new course to the pilot. I only hoped that the aircraft would hang together and get us home on three engines. We appeared to have cleared the main flak area and were heading in the right direction for home, but I felt very vulnerable down at 7,000 feet as the other returning bombers would be flying home about 18,000 feet. It was going to be a long solitary journey home but I was pleased we were doing this and had not been forced to make for the Russian lines which were not far to the east, as one never knew what to expect when flying in the vicinity of the Red Army.

The damage to our aircraft was extensive but with a bit of luck we felt we could make it back to the United Kingdom. The captain was magnificent in his handling of the situation and this could be said of the whole crew who kept their heads and in no way panicked under these desperate conditions.

Our set operator, Flight Sergeant Kelly, even with all his injuries had climbed back to his desk and was operating the H2S equipment. Although it was draughty and cold in my bomb aimer's compartment I was desperate to do as much map reading as possible to ensure that we avoided running over flak areas where we would be vulnerable to light Ack-Ack fire which could reach up to about 8,000 feet. I knew we would be safe from flak when we crossed over the Allied army lines but we would still have to be on the alert for fighters although these appeared to be few in number. It seemed a very long journey back to the coast but on reaching it I pinpointed our position and passed it to the navigator and breathed a great sigh of relief as we headed over the North Sea.

I thought it safe to go back from the bomb aimer's compartment in the nose to the navigation position where I suggested to Flight Sergeant Kelly that I might give him a break and operate his H2S set, but this brave, brave young man, although looking quite pale and ill, looked up at me and said:

'I feel not too bad now, so I will just continue as we haven't far to go.'

I returned to the nose to try and pinpoint our position when we reached the English coast. Oh, what a wonderful feeling as our aircraft struggled across the English coast and we headed towards Oakington with everybody keeping their fingers crossed that our wheels would come down and our undercarriage was not too badly damaged.

The captain had alerted Oakington by R/T of our predicament and fire engines and ambulance were standing by in case we had to make an emergency landing and also to ensure that our wounded crew member would be transferred to hospital immediately.

The Air Traffic Controller gave us an immediate clearance for landing and as I sat in the second pilot's seat and watched the runway come into view and heard the undercarriage go down I felt we were nearly there as we skipped over the hedges and on to the end of the runway and as we screeched on to the tarmac surface and the undercarriage held as we rolled forward along the runway. All the crew sighed with relief as we turned off the runway and taxied towards the aircraft parking area at the hangars where the ambulance and fire engine were in attendance.

As our aircraft stopped and the engines were cut I felt as if we had escaped from the jaws of death. The rear door was opened and the steps were put down and we all trooped out. I remember I felt like kissing the ground as I got to the bottom of the steps, but there were the station commander, medical officer, squadron commander and a few others all there to welcome us home. Flight Sergeant Kelly was whisked away in the ambulance on his way to Ely Hospital where I hoped the medics would be able to patch him up and save him from any permanent damage to his leg. It was quite dark as I tried to get a good look at our damaged aircraft but one could see it was extensive. (Next morning I was to find that the Ack-Ack shells had torn more than a hundred holes of varying sizes into the fuselage of our aircraft.)

At debriefing that night I was to lace my coffee with a little more than the usual tot of rum and oh how wonderful it was to see the relief on the faces of our Skipper and the whole crew. They were all magnificent and I was honoured and privileged to have flown with such a fine crew. I think their experience played a great part in our survival. The handling of such a damaged aircraft by Flight Lieutenant Phillips was wonderful to behold and certainly played the major part in our survival.

The debriefing officers were to assure us that the raid had been a complete success and much damage had been done to the synthetic oil works, so maybe my first Deputy Master Bomber raid had achieved its objective although crews had experienced heavy flak and some interference from German night fighters. After having told our complete story at debriefing I did not need any rocking when back in my room I turned in and was at peace with the world.

A few weeks after this raid, Flight Sergeant Kelly was to receive the award of the Conspicuous Gallantry Medal. The whole squadron was delighted with his award and I was proud to have flown with such a brave courageous young man whose injuries by this time were beginning to heal and it was thought that he would not be left with any permanent injury.

My baptism in the Deputy Master role was very much more hectic than I had ever dreamed. I knew well that Master Bombers could expect to have narrow escapes but I did not expect to get such a quick reminder over Bohlen. Here was I thinking that the war was nearly over and just failing to get myself shot from the sky with the end of this conflict in sight; I said a little prayer and hoped that my good luck would carry me through.

In no way was my squadron commander going to let my thoughts dwell on Bohlen because as soon as I awoke I was to find I was back on operations that very night, but this time as a Primary Visual Marker with my own crew. I dragged myself out of bed and across to Intelligence to find the target was Chemnitz, so another long haul to East Germany in support of the advancing Red Army.

From the previous night I knew there was a considerable amount of cloud in the Chemnitz area, so hoped it had not increased as I very much wanted to be able to mark the target visually as there was over 700 bombers on the operation. We took off at 17.00 hours and did not encounter any opposition en route to Chemnitz but as we approached the city about 20.30 hours there was enormous cloud cover over the whole area and in no way was I going to be able to mark the target visually so to my great disappointment it had to be a Wanganui (sky marking attack). I thought on this occasion that with more than 700 bombers over the city there was a reasonable chance that the attack would hit home at supplies, communications, and any troops that might be garrisoned in the city.

There appeared to be a moderate amount of heavy flak reaching around the flight level of the bombers but I saw only one very large flash just after leaving the target, but was too far off to make any guess as to whether it might have been one of our bombers. The sky markers did not appear to be drifting too rapidly and I could see no reason why the majority of bombs would not fall on the city. For our crew it was home, Ken, and don't spare the revs, and with not a German night fighter in sight our captain was calling Oakington for landing instructions at about 15 minutes past midnight.

During the last few months of the European War it was so wonderful to see the great change that had come over the squadron aircrew as losses were now down to about 1% for the Command and the chances of survival had greatly increased.

(above) Visual bomb aimers of
[ ] Pathfinder Squadron,
[Warb]ington, with the 8 Group
[bom]bing shield. Spring 1945.
(ba[ck row, left to right) Flt Lt
[Bar]tley, DFC, Flt Lt Macdonald,
[ ], Flt Lt Taylor, DFC, DFM,
[Fl]t Greenaway, DFC,
[Fl]t Epstein, DFC
(fro[nt row, left to right) Flt
[Lt M]aitland, DFC (author) Sqn
[Ldr] White DFC, Flt Lt Berry
[DFC] and bar. Note the happy
[face]s as their long war was
[near]ing its end.

(rig[ht)] Pforzheim, viewed from
[8,0]00 feet on the night of 23/
[24t]h February 1945. Master
[Bom]ber for this attack was
[Capt]ain E. Swales, DFC, SAAF,
[who] won a posthumous VC on
[this] raid.

There was a great feeling of victory in the air and spirits were high as everyone thought the defeat of the Third Reich was at hand.

Ken Rawson, being an Aussie, wanted to see as much of the United Kingdom as possible, both from the air and on the ground, so we seldom had a dull moment. He would volunteer to fly the station Air Speed Oxford Transport aircraft at every opportunity and I would go along as navigator when we were required to ferry aircrew from Oakington to other stations. If we were not required for operations usually we were off duty and often we could be found on Rawson's motor bike burning up the miles on the country roads or more sedately in the small Ford car I had managed to acquire cheaply from one of the Aussie boys who was due to return to Australia. I was pleased to have some means of transport as we were fortunate in receiving a small petrol ration and this allowed us to visit the golf course, Cambridge and the surrounding countryside. I enjoyed walking along the banks of the Cam and visiting colleges like King's, Trinity and many of the others which never failed to interest me historically and architecturally. There were many fine pubs and hostelries in the area and places like the Baron of Beef and the Pike and Eel were great favourites with aircrew as were the dances held in the Guildhall.

There always seemed to be a good-natured running battle in progress between the city's undergraduates and aircrew. Undergraduates would be found tied to lamp standards, their gowns having been used for tethering while others would have gowns burned with cigarettes as they visited pubs, but not to be outdone they would make attacks on aircrew cars by removing the wheels and leaving them jacked up in the car park. It was not uncommon for the citizens of Cambridge to observe as they walked to work in the mornings things like WAAF panties flying from spires or flag poles on buildings. I often wondered if we had steeplejacks in the RAF because many of the high places that flew the ladies' underwear looked quite inaccessible from the ground and a certain amount of quite dangerous climbing would have been necessary to reach the chosen points.

Although I liked to get away from Oakington and service life from time to time I did like the officers' mess where there was always something going on and the bar was a very pleasant place to drink and where later in the evenings there were always plenty of games like Colonel Puff and a great variety of songs being sung, so there was never a dull moment and often the parties went on into the small hours of the morning much to the annoyance of those who were in bed and wanted to sleep.

Although at this time victory seemed assured, in no way after my recent experience over the skies of Bohlen was I to consider the war was finished because as long as we kept going to German targets and the defences kept flinging ack-ack shells into the air and we kept trying to avoid them then there would always be a shell that would knock a bomber out of the sky. I would know the war was over when we could fly over the Ruhr and find that there were no shells bursting alongside our aircraft. I would know then that Germany had surrendered.

Sir Arthur Harris was taking no chances with the Germans and he ordered about 350 bombers to attack communications at Worms on the West side of the Rhine on 21st February. Obviously a raid in support of the advancing Allied Armies approaching this area. This was a night raid and as cloud covered the target, sky marking had to be used, but I felt sure that with such a large number of bombers communications in the area would be devastated.

A daylight raid on the 27th saw us again in the Deputy Master Bomber role when over 450 bombers attacked Mainz where it was quite difficult to assess the extent of the damage due to cloud. This place had been attacked on three previous occasions so now after this fourth main force attack we were not to return so I imagine Sir Arthur was quite pleased with results achieved. The flak was not too heavy and we were to escape without any aircraft damage and this was to be our last raid for the month of February 1945.

Our first raid in March was a long haul to the town of Dessau which would be important for the supply of materials to the Germans facing the advancing Red Army. We encountered slight flak and although there was a lot of cloud I felt certain that the town was hit with a large number of bombs.

Sir Arthur Harris had so many bombers in his Command they could now be sent in large numbers to continue the Commander-in-Chief's main aim – the area bombing of the German cities – and still have bombers to spare for raids in direct support of the armies. Bomber aircraft could now be ranged at will with devastating attacks wherever Harris thought they were required, so it was not surprising that we were primary visual marker for a night raid on the city of Hamburg on 8th March. I thought I had finished with this target in 1943 after the Battle of Hamburg, but things did not stand still and, as I have said, previously the Germans were adept at improvisation and rebuilding so an industrial place like Hamburg would always need a bit of attention and on this occasion it was the submarine building yards that was to have the bombers' attention. The cloud was quite thick in the area but with quite big gaps, it was possible to see the ground and get the target indicators more or less on the aiming point. On leaving the Hamburg area it appeared that the main force bombers were crashing bombs down on the markers which I hoped were in the right place. I was quite pleased to get away from the city which seemed to be producing quite a flak barrage.

Just before midday on 11th March our crew were briefed for a daylight raid to Essen and we had been given the Deputy Master Bomber role. The whole crew was pleased we had reached such a high standard of efficiency where our superiors thought us fit for this role on such an important target as Essen.

My experience of Essen was that its defences were second only to those of Berlin and on occasions I had felt their heavy flak barrage was every bit as concentrated as that of the capital. Essen had always been a place much feared by air crew as this large industrial city, the biggest in the Ruhr was the home of the giant Krupps works, or what was now left of them. It also had contained much light and heavy industry, but much of this must have disappeared after such a long and continuous bombardment. It had never been an easy place to bomb but I

156

knew at this stage of the war that their defences were not as fierce or on the scale they had been when I first visited the city in May 1943. Nevertheless it was still a place requiring the greatest respect.

I was quite familiar with the city as since joining Pathfinder Force I had visited it on a night marking sortie on 23rd October 1944, a daylight marking sortie on 25th October and another night marking trip on 12th December 1944. I had experienced the fury of its defences when visiting it on a Halifax aircraft in May 1943. It was not surprising on this occasion when I arrived at Intelligence to study photographs and target maps that I felt I had seen quite a bit of this previously, so all I hoped for now was for a clear view of the city and the aiming point which was in the old part of the city, in fact not far from what was left of Krupps works.

At briefing the weather forecast was giving quite good weather in the Ruhr and it looked as if this was going to be a good opportunity to prove ourselves in the Deputy Master Bomber role. As over 900 bombers were being dispatched on this attack it was imperative that as we were marking first that our markers should be on the aiming point.

We took off at 14.00 hours and arrived over the target area just before 16.00 hours to find there were only small amounts of cloud and the ground details in the city were showing up quite clearly. As we approached Essen on a southerly course there was a wonderful view of the whole city spread out below me and what I saw was quite frightening. There were heaps upon heaps of rubble with thousands of buildings razed to the ground, some with walls still standing stood out like pillars of resistance. I estimated that at least 50% of the city was destroyed or partially destroyed and it looked as if what had not been burned had been blasted into rubble. For once I thought I felt sorry for the Germans living in this ghost city, then my mind strayed to the days of 1943 when their defences terrified aircrew and claimed many young lives; my sympathy was soon to evaporate.

I was particularly pleased to have this opportunity of seeing this city which had been so terrifying to so many aircrews of

157

Bomber Command throughout the war lying there below me looking quite subdued and only offering token resistance with a few anti-aircraft shells bursting around the Bombers.

I guided Ken on to the aiming point which I could see quite clearly from some way off. A nice straight uninterrupted run into the point of release as my;

'Left, left,'

'Steady,'

routine got the aiming point moving down the reflector plate of the bombsight and it was,

'Bomb doors open,' and

'Bombs gone,'

as the release point was reached. It was then,

'Bomb doors closed,'

as we pushed on through the target area and as we started to climb I could see the red target markers cascading on to the aiming point and it looked as if before they even hit the ground the main force bombs were crashing through the roofs of buildings in the built-up area and others were crashing on to the still standing buildings of the Krupps works. Seldom had I seen so clearly bombs penetrating and exploding on and in buildings.

As we climbed away to take up our station circling the target and watching the waves of bombers go through the target, the Master Bomber was instructing the main force bombers by R/T to bomb the target indicators and as more waves of bombers came through the target was kept marked by the Pathfinder backer-up aircraft dropping their green markers around the aiming point.

We circled above the main stream of bombers and watched each wave of bombers approach and drop their bombs and soon the whole area around the aiming point became completely saturated and Krupps was also taking a pounding with some bombs that appeared to be undershooting the marked aiming point. I had waited a long time to see a raid of this intensity moving through a Ruhr target so smoothly and with very little opposition. I was convinced the Germans had reached the end of the road.

It took about 25 minutes for all the waves to go through and as we made our final orbit, the Master called us to confirm the raid was over and it was time to go home. Never could I have thought in my wildest dreams in 1943 that we would be able to spend 25 minutes over Essen without having been shot from the sky. Jack passed over our new course to Ken and our nose was pointed towards the United Kingdom.

As we made our way home I felt we had proved ourselves in the Deputy Master role, because they did not come much bigger than Essen. But things were not to be all that easy. As we crossed the Belgian coast north of Dunkirk we had come down to about 8,000 feet to observe some ground detail when the Germans, who were still occupying Dunkirk which had been bypassed by the Allied armies, opened fire with several anti-aircraft shells which burst around our tail causing some damage in the area of the rear gun turret, wounding our rear gunner in his leg. At the same time the aircraft seemed to take a dive towards the sea and it took the captain a few seconds to bring it under control, but by this time we were only about a thousand feet above the water. Luckily for us the controls had not been too badly damaged and he was able to maintain it straight and level for our homeward flight over the North Sea.

Alan Camlin, our rear gunner, had been taken from the rear turret and was now on the stretcher with his wounds bandaged with wound dressings. He was bearing up bravely as we sped towards the English coast at low level making a bee line straight for our base at Oakington. On approaching base, Ken requested priority landing and we made a direct approach and fortunately had no difficulty in landing. The ambulance was awaiting our arrival and Alan was soon on board and on his way to the RAF Hospital at Ely. We made an inspection of the tail of our aircraft and I think we all thought that we had been lucky to escape more serious damage.

I felt so pleased that our raid had been a success but felt so damned angry that the Bosche had been able to hit us and wound our gunner and I only hoped that Alan's wound would not be too serious.

At debriefing the squadron commander was to congratulate the crew on their performance as the attack had been a complete success.

This was the last time that RAF heavy bombers were to go to Essen although I did not know this at the time. Looking back on it at the end of the war, I was grateful that we had been given the Deputy Master Bomber role and that I had been able to see so much of the attack on a city that had so often struck terror into my heart and also into the hearts of so many of my fellow aircrew.

The view I had of that subdued city of Essen on this, its final, bombing raid by Royal Air Force Bomber Command on 11th March 1945 will always be imprinted on my mind and I will always remember the many thousands of young men who had fallen to the city's defences during the 28 raids carried out by heavy bombers on Germany's industrial capital. Essen had truly reaped the whirlwind.

By the middle of March 1945 the news coming from Europe was that the victorious Allied armies were advancing on all fronts and that the Wehrmacht were pulling further back into what was left of their homeland with the Allies on their heels.

From the briefing map showing the position of the Allied armies it was quite clear that a large pincer movement was in progress to completely surround the Ruhr and the main industrial part of Germany.

The First Canadian Army was fighting its way through Holland and was pushing on towards the German North Sea ports of Emden and Wilhelmshaven. The American Ninth Army having negotiated the Rhine in the Weser area was now across in force and advancing in the direction of the city of Hanover and on their left flank was the British Second Army advancing towards the Weser River in the direction of Luneberg Heath.

Further south the Americans had established a good bridgehead over the Rhine a little south of Bonn and troops and armour were across in force and were now on their way north in two separate pushes. One was heading for the Harz Mountains, the other towards Lippstadt to link up with the Ninth Army advancing on Hanover.

During this period it was very difficult to keep up with troop movements as positions were changing very quickly as the advance continued.

On the Eastern Front the Red Army was advancing on Berlin and other Russian troops were advancing towards the River Elbe.

It was wonderful to see the speed of advance of the Allied armies and that the casualty rate was nothing like it was in France in the First World War. So perhaps the continuous bombing of Germany by the RAF and USAAF was now paying dividends and Sir Arthur Harris had achieved one of his greatest objectives. Perhaps the thousands of aircrew who had been killed in the skies over Germany had not died in vain for without their sacrifice it is pretty certain that Army casualties would have been enormous and the advance would have been a much slower affair.

CHAPTER XI

Victory in Sight

The Commander-in-Chief with about 1500 bombers in his Command was still keeping his aircrew busy as the German defences grew weaker and one tended to have some sympathy with the German civilian population who were taking a terrible beating and living in appalling conditions amongst the rubble of their cities. Harris ranged the bombers over a wide variety of targets such as oil refineries, oil storage tanks, synthetic oil plants and any other relative oil industries. It was little wonder that the Bosche was desperately short of fuel. Communications, marshalling yards, submarine building yards and raids in support of the Army such as troop concentrations, gun emplacements were all commonplace as were raids on towns in the East in support of the Eastern Front. The area bombing of cities was still continuing so there was to be no let up by Sir Arthur Harris as his bombers hit at every corner of what was left of the Third Reich and the Allied armies' squeeze on the Fatherland grew tighter and tighter.

Our Master Bomber raid on Essen must have impressed as we were given the same role for raids to Hamburg on the night of 14th March and a daylight to Recklinghausen on the 20th. Both raids were successful and we experienced little flak on either trip. The gunners did not report any fighter activity and considering these were Master Bomber sorties the inactivity of the German defences pleased us immensely, but if we were to think that all the defences of Germany had been greatly reduced or had run out of ammunition we were to be rudely awakened as we were ordered to carry out the Deputy Master Bomber role on a daylight raid to Hamburg on the last day of March and much to our surprise were to given quite a hot reception with a heavy flak barrage being put up by the defences of this much bombed city. The attack was forced home and proved quite successful, but I was to feel that there was still quite a bit of vigilance required especially as a Deputy Master Bomber if we were not to fall foul of an anti-aircraft shell in this final stage of the war and I only hoped our luck would hold.

The beginning of April saw the whole free world rejoicing at the reports of the advancing Allied armies as they moved further and further into Germany. They now had the Ruhr surrounded and were pushing on towards Bremen and the Elbe, The Red Army was on its way to Berlin and also advancing towards the Elbe to meet up with the Americans and British.

Many German troops were now fleeing westward towards the advancing British and American troops rather than fall into Russian hands, as they hoped for more correct POW treatment from the Western Allies. They certainly would get very little sympathy from the Russians as they would never forget the atrocities the Bosche had committed in Russia.

During this period Bomber Command were particularly active on communications, oil supplies and troop concentrations. The Red Army's advance was being supported by the continued bombing of towns and cities in the path of their advance where it was known that German troops, supplies and communications were aiding the Germans on the Eastern Front.

By this stage in the war the German armed forces were desperately short of fuel for aircraft, tanks and motorised vehicles and Sir Arthur Harris was ensuring that any fuel supplies of any consequence were receiving the attention of his bombers. It was therefore not surprising that 7 Squadron were ordered to mark for a fairly big raid on Harburg, the town that lay across the River Elbe from Hamburg. Apparently there was a fairly large oil storage depot in the town which was not to be there very long after the bombers arrived. 7 Squadron marked the target accurately and by the time we were turning for home the whole depot was burning from end to end and another nail was hammered into the German coffin.

We were ordered back to this area on 8th April when in the Deputy Master Bomber role we were to dive through the broken cloud to mark the submarine building yards at Hamburg. This city which had received so many large and damaging raids was still managing to put up some sort of semblance of resistance in the way of a medium flak barrage so as we orbited the target and watched the main force bombers go through I was ever vigilant as were the others in the crew. The occasional rattle of shrapnel on the underside of the fuselage would make the heart beat a little faster and I prayed the 'Reaper' would not cut us down at this late stage of the war. As this, our last raid on Hamburg, ended I was pleased to leave this city of rubble and never ending flak barrages and make for the quiet of the sky over the North Sea.

I had been to the city of Hamburg five times and on the last two occasions in the Deputy Master Bomber role, so I had probably seen the last raid on this doomed city. A city like Hamburg that had struck fear into my heart and into the hearts of many aircrew and its defences had claimed many hundreds of my Bomber Command comrades. I hoped the Allied ground forces would soon reach this city and spare the civil population from any further aerial bombardment. Hamburg had reaped the whirlwind and what a whirlwind.

Air Vice Marshal Bennett was a great believer in keeping his crews in Pathfinder Force at the peak of efficiency and it was therefore the group policy that as much flying training as possible should be carried out when time was available and weather was suitable between operational sorties. This policy of continuation training was carried out right up to the end of the war as my log book shows our crew having carried out 13.45 hours in April and 16.25 in March 1945.

To keep pilots and bomb aimers up to scratch a Group Bombing Shield was competed for each month and awarded to the squadron in the group which achieved the best bombing results on the practice bombing ranges. I believe 7 Squadron held this shield at the end of April 1945. Our crew quite enjoyed the continuation training and were always keen we should get

164

good results on the practice bombing range. From my own point of view I loved flying and was prepared to fly anytime, day or night, but preferred it not to be bombing sorties over Germany. Having been connected with civil flying prior to the RAF I wanted to return after the war, but wanted to go back in some flying capacity, so I was anxious to get as much flying experience as possible as this could only be good for my future career.

Now that aircrew were sensing the end of hostilities their minds were turning the post war careers and those interested in civil aviation were now studying for pilot licences or civil air navigation certificates.

It was an early lunch on the 10th April and briefing directly afterwards for an attack on the city of Leipzig. This was one of the few supply bases left to the Germans in their attempts to bolster up their crumbling Eastern Front as the Red Army drove on relentlessly towards the Elbe. The American armies from the south were now pushing on towards the Leipzig area.

At briefing all the crews seemed very cheery and everyone believed that victory was now very close, but many like myself felt quite apprehensive as experience had taught us that where there was defensive armament there would always be casualties, so we would just keep our fingers crossed and hope that although our crew were again in the Deputy Master Bomber role that the time we were to spend over the target would not be too hazardous.

We took off from Oakington at 15.00 hours with good weather conditions en route and we were over the target at about 18.20 hours where the weather was also good and we had no difficulty in pinpointing and marking our aiming point in the city. There was a moderate amount of flak coming from the ground defences, but most of it was falling short of our height and I sincerely hoped that it would stay at that level.

As we climbed away from the city to take up our orbiting position above the flight level of the main force bombers who were now being instructed by the Master Bomber to attack the red markers which were the ones we had just dropped, so like us, he must have thought they were in the correct position. By this

165

HP Halifax B.III, MZ759, NP-Q of 158 Squadron, hit by flak and afire over Gladbach (Ruhr) on 24th March 1945. It crashed within minutes of this shot.

The aftermath. An aerial view of the devastation in Cologne, April 1945.

time the first wave of bombers were dropping their bombs fairly accurately around the target markers and the whole attack looked quite concentrated. As we circled overhead and watched several waves of bombers drop their bombs and fly on through the target I could see no casualties, so hoped it would remain like this. I was wondering if perhaps this would be the last time I would be looking down on a scene like this as the bombs crashed into the built-up area.

I thought there must be many German troops in transit and probably large numbers of the civilian population who would be fleeing the advancing Russians and would also be on their way through the town. This was probably one of the few important targets left in this diminishing Third Reich and as we turned for home and I took a last look at Leipzig I was to wonder why this stupid man Hitler did not put these people out of their agony by surrendering this very day, as I suspected the last chapters of the war were now being played out and Hitler's Reich was now living on borrowed time.

As we sped westwards towards the Allied Army Lines there was not a German fighter to be seen in the sky and the flak batteries along our route were silent and I wondered if the killing skies of Germany had been subdued, but I would not admit this to myself till such time as the ceasefire had been arranged. It was over our armies on the ground, then over the North Sea and Ken was calling up Oakington at about 21.40 hours and soon after he was putting our wheels on to the runway for yet another good landing.

It was on to debriefing for our coffee and rum and then quite a detailed debriefing as in the Deputy Master role we were longer over the target and were therefore able to observe much more than others and it was quite important that debriefing officers got as much detail out of the Master and Deputy Master crews as possible.

I arrived at the mess in time to grab myself a pint at the bar and then it was a hearty meal in the dining hall. It was so wonderful to see the happy cheery faces of men who had fought so long and so hard as they sat at their meal and could sense that

167

a great victory was at hand, but just when was the question.

By about mid-April the good news coming out of Europe confirmed that the German economy was definitely in ruins and the Allied advance was continuing with German forces surrendering in their thousands. The German forces in the Ruhr area were in a hopeless position and 21st Infantry Divisions consisting of 350,000 men had surrendered to the Allies.

Allies in the southern and central areas of Germany were reporting swift advances with few casualties and thousands of Germans surrendering. The only enemy troops not giving up were some fanatical Nazis who were hoping for some kind of miracle by Hitler.

News from the Eastern Front was the Red Army advance was still pushing the Germans back and they were poised for an all-out attack on the city of Berlin. The Germans were fighting a very desperate rear guard action and were inflicting large casualties on the Russians, but they themselves were not without heavy losses. Red Army troops were now approaching the River Elbe on its east side and the Americans on its west side and it looked as if the link-up would come pretty soon.

It now looked as if the final Battle for Berlin would not be long delayed as the Russians were either on or across the Oder and fighting the Germans in their defensive positions just east of their capital. The German armies left fighting were now in a very desperate position which looked as if it could only get worse.

As more and more reports from the various fronts in Europe came to hand and the BBC broadcast the good news the whole British nation could now see that victory was imminent and that the long years of struggle and sacrifice to defeat Hitler's Third Reich were now ending. A great feeling of joy and relief was emerging as the whole nation felt that the German surrender was not likely to be long delayed.

On 13th April we were again in the Deputy Master Bomber role for a night attack on Kiel. Ken Rawson and myself were getting a bit annoyed that we had not been given a Master Bomber attack I believed he had tackled the squadron

168

commander on the subject and had been told that we would be given the Master role in the near future.

I had never been to Kiel before but knew it as a very important port and naval base with lots of docks and shipyards and was a city that had been attacked many times, being one of the first targets to be hit in the early part of the war. Since 27th/28th February 1942 it had seen eight main force raids from the heavy bombers, some of them involving large numbers of aircraft. As recently as 9th April 1945 the German warship *Admiral Scheer* had been attacked from the air and was capsized in the harbour, so it looked as if there was quite a bit of naval activity in and around the port.

Our aiming point for the attack was in the dock area including the submarine pens. The take-off from Oakington was scheduled for 19.30 hours and we calculated time on target to be 22.30 hours and a further three hours for the return journey. I was sincerely hoping that this place would not be too troublesome with a large flak barrage as I would hate to get knocked about at this late stage of the war. The route to and from the target was nearly all over sea so on arrival at the target I was pleasantly surprised to find only small amounts of flak but was disappointed to find so much heavy cloud about and was

Pathfinder Barons: From left to right: Grp Capt John Searby, DSO, DFC, Wg Cdr S.P. 'Pat' Daniels, DSO, DFC; Grp Capt R.W.P. Collings, DSO, DFC; Grp Capt T.G. 'Hamish' Mahaddie, DSO, DFC, AFC; AVM D.C.T. Bennett, CE, CBE, DSO

therefore unable to mark the target visually so we needed sky markers. The sky markers did not seem to be drifting too fast so I hoped all the bombs going through the cloud were hitting home on the dock areas.

As the last wave went through and we turned our nose towards the North Sea and England I wondered how many more attacks before it would be all over. We landed back at Oakington at 01.30 on 14th April on this which was to be our penultimate raid although we did not know this at the time.

On 16th April the Chiefs of Staff formally decreed the ending of area bombing, but Bomber Command were not to be inactive for the last few weeks of the war and we were called upon to carry out a raid to Bremen in support of our advancing armies and we were to have the primary visual marker role. It was a straightforward attack with little or no flak either on the target or enroute and was completed in 4 hours 20 minutes.

I remember as Ken Rawson closed down our four engines I wondered if this would be our last raid. Although I did not know this at the time, something told me that for us the war was over, but felt I must see the Germans surrender before I would believe that we would not require to return. I did not think I would be like Napoleon and weep if I did not have to return, but it was never far from my mind that there was still a war to be won in the Far East.

CHAPTER XII

Victory in Europe

The final weeks of April saw everyone on the squadron full of high spirits and many of them quite full of beer at times, but who could blame them as they awaited the final surrender of Germany? The news from the army fronts in Europe was of many victories and thousands of German troops surrendering as the advance continued. The Red Army was near the outskirts of Berlin and the final battle for the city was in progress.

On 22nd April the squadron flew a mercy mission to Rotterdam to drop food to the Dutch people who by this time were desperately short of anything to eat. It was wonderful to see the liberated Dutch people wave and acknowledge the sacks of food that we dropped on to the marked out dropping zones. It was also wonderful that our last mission to Europe had been one of mercy and the recipients were people who had suffered so much under the Nazis.

On 25th April we were given the news that the Americans had joined up with the Red Army at Torgau on the River Elbe. On 2nd May the German Army surrendered Berlin as the Red Army troops poured into the city.

On 3rd May approaches were made to Field Marshal Montgomery for the surrender of all the German forces in north-west Germany and this surrender was signed at Luneberg Heath on 5th May 1945 and the final surrender of all German forces in the West was signed in Rheims by Colonel-General Jodl and representatives of General Eisenhower, the Supreme Allied Commander in Europe. A further surrender was demanded by the Russians and this was

171

Heligoland, May 1945.

Hamburg on the day of its surrender, 3rd May 1945.

Aftermath. Essen on 18th May, 1945.

arranged for Berlin on 8th May with Germans, Allies and Russians all attending.

Churchill announced that 8th May would be celebrated as Victory in Europe Day and this great victory was to be celebrated in the Allied capitals throughout the world.

I had started a seven day period of leave on the 7th and wondered if I should celebrate VE Day in London as some of my crew were going to the capital for the celebrations. I made my way to London with them but on reaching the city and seeing the crowds beginning to assemble I decided that I would make my way to King's Cross Station and head for Scotland. As I boarded the train I could hear the crowds singing Land of Hope and Glory and Rule Britannia could be heard echoing around the station as servicemen and servicewomen joined with civilians in dancing to celebrate this very special victory. Their joy and relief was so wonderful to see and it was not surprising as we had been a very long time at war.

I hoped to be home early on VE Day to spend it with my folks and the bonnie lass who later was to become my wife.

As I settled down on the train and we pulled away from the station I began to think how lucky I was to have survived the war and I wiped a tear from my eye as I thought of my comrades who would not be going home and for the parents and relatives, wives and sweethearts who perhaps would this day be mourning a loved one who had died in battle. I hoped our nation would forever honour and never forget these young, high spirited, courageous and brave young men who had given their all in the cause of freedom.

My VE Day was to be spent on the golf course followed in the evening with a few glasses of that famous old Scottish spirit shared with my 'Ain Folk'.

CHAPTER XIII

Tributes and Achievements

In the last chapter of my book I would like to pay tribute to Marshal of the Royal Air Force Sir Arthur Harris who commanded RAF Bomber Command from February 1942 till the end of the war, 8th May 1945.

I would also like to sum up very briefly what I believe to have been the achievements of the bomber offensive as seen through the eyes of a bomb aimer.

Finally I would like to treat as a separate achievement the part that the offensive played on the morale of our enemies, the peoples of the occupied countries of Europe and on our own citizens of the United Kingdom.

Sir Arthur Harris was in his late forties when he took over as Commander-in-Chief of RAF Bomber Command at the end of February 1942. Here was a man who was expertly qualified to direct the operations of this important Command.

He had finished the First World War as a major with the Air Force Cross and decided to remain in the Royal Air Force. Between the wars he was always particularly interested in bomber operations and commanded several bomber squadrons. While on these squadrons he showed great interest in the development of bombing equipment including bombsights and was forever endeavouring to improve bombing techniques. Early in the Second World War he was given command of Number 5 Group of RAF Bomber Command and it was during this period that he became known for the very efficient methods he used in directing the squadrons in his group at a time when the Command had to do its best with a limited number of aircraft available. I think he would be remembered for his efforts during this period and it would have some bearing when it came to appoint him as the new Commander-in-Chief of Bomber Command.

He was a man completely dedicated to the bomber operations, who fully believed that given the requisite number of aircraft he could defeat Germany by air power alone. He was a brave leader and was never afraid to take decisions. He was absolutely ruthless in pursuing his adopted policy of the area bombardment of German towns and cities. He was never to deviate to any great extent from his area bombing policy except at the command of Eisenhower before, during and for some time after D-Day, but as soon as he could escape, or have this commitment reduced or as more bombers became available, it was back to the punishment of the German towns and cities. Perhaps if Harris could have had 1500 bombers available to him in 1942 as he had in 1945 then perhaps who knows with the help of the US Eighth Air Force he might have bombed the Reich into surrender. I do not think we will ever be able to assess just how near Harris came to achieving his objective, but he must have gone a long way towards his aim and perhaps was much nearer than many historian seem to think.

I spent a long time in Bomber Command squadrons during the war but I was never to meet our Commander-in-Chief, although, like the great majority of aircrew on his Command I was to have the greatest admiration and respect for this great leader. He never failed to identify himself completely with the interests of his front line operational aircrew. His attitude that we should hit the Bosche hard and often where it hurt most appealed to his aircrew and ground staff alike. He appeared to have the ability to make each person under this command believe that he or she was playing an integral part in the bomber offensive. Many were the stories that reached squadron level about the exploits of Harris. Some could be believed, but others had been greatly distorted or invented by his admirers but on the whole these tales did much to enhance his popularity.

It mattered little to aircrew in the front line squadrons that at

176

his headquarters at High Wycombe he was known by his Staff Officers to be harsh, blunt, sharp of tongue and hated anyone to disagree with him. What did matter to them was that he was prepared to fight to see that they got the best aircraft and equipment with which to fight as he was well aware of the very many problems and hazards that lay in the hostile skies of Germany.

No aircrew were ever in doubt as to the objectiveness of Sir Arthur Harris and it says much for this man as a leader that in 1943 when the squadron casualties were at their worst and only about 10% of aircrew were surviving a tour of 30 operations that the morale remained high and only a very small number of aircrew were to fall by the wayside because of lack of moral fibre.

Never did I during my service on operational squadrons hear anyone at anytime say an unkind word about their Commander-in-Chief. Harris was our leader and his policy was our policy and where he sent us and what he decided needed bombing was good enough for his aircrews, as we knew we would be hitting the Bosche where it hurt most, probably right in the middle of his cities.

In British homes, factories, workshops, in bars and pubs the people knew the name of Harris and it was not unusual to hear remarks like. 'Wonder where Butch is sending his bombers tonight?,' as the bombers climbed away from their airfield for yet another bombing raid.

To me Sir Arthur Harris was a great leader and a great wartime commander and even if he did have his ups and downs with his superiors and was a bit hard on his staff officers, and many historians since the war have been most critical of him, he must have had great qualities to build up and maintain at the peak of efficiency such a complex Command and in so doing retain the complete trust and admiration of all who served in Bomber Command.

To try and assess accurately the overall achievements of the RAF bomber offensive throughout the Second World War is probably well nigh impossible due to many factors that have been overlooked or forgotten and statistics which at times are not

177

all accurate. Figures were often adjusted by the Germans to suit their own propaganda purposes.

Instead of bombarding the reader with a very large number of figures and statistics which I feel sure would make the mind boggle, I have decided it would be better to write down what I and probably other members of aircrews thought we were achieving in bombing German towns and cities and what our efforts were contributing to the overall war effort.

The offensive forced the Germans to employ many thousands of men and women in a very large and sophisticated defence system to try and combat the aerial bombardment. Many personnel were employed in Germany and the occupied countries on the early warning radar systems, communication systems for ground and air defences; very large numbers were employed on the operation of searchlights, anti-aircraft guns and all the associated equipment required to keep these weapons at operational readiness.

To maintain an efficient fighter force of several hundred fighter aircraft needed many highly trained aircrew and all the necessary skilled ground staff to keep aircraft serviceable and to run the day to day services required to operate modern military airfields. Most of these people employed on the actual defensive weapons would be fairly skilled technically and to have them tied down to this defensive role when no doubt the armed forces of the Reich would have welcomed them on their front line operations must have been annoying.

Added to the manpower required in the defensive system there were the thousands, perhaps less technical personnel, such as police, air raid wardens, firemen, ambulance men and gangs of labourers required to dig out dead and wounded and to clear rubble and maintain road and rail communications. There would be the large number of tradesmen such as joiners, plumbers, electricians who would be permanently employed in trying to keep the essential services going to homes, workshops, factories and rebuilding or repairing property damaged in raids. Engineers would be required in large numbers to repair or replace plant and machinery damaged at places of work.

Air Vice Marshal Don Bennett; Marshal of the RAF Lord Trenchard and Lord Cherwell in the RAF Wyton's Officers' Mess.

Sir Arthur Harris's main aim in the area bombing of towns and cities was to destroy as far as possible the German industrial potential to wage war. To succeed in this aim was not an easy task as factories, foundries, workshops and in fact all work places that were producing anything that was important to the German war effort would be targets for the bombers to destroy and disrupt. In attacking the industry in areas of population it was inevitable that the homes of the workers would receive a great amount of damage and when homes are burned or blasted this causes great disorganisation amongst the workers and results in thousand upon thousand of man hours being lost.

As the war progressed and more and more bombers became available to Bomber Command the Commander-in-Chief was able to attack cities more frequently and although the Germans were known to be very resilient the weight of bombs being dropped in the latter part of the war was to take its toll on German industrial output. I think most aircrew like myself believed that if we could hit German industry hard enough and often enough the German ability to wage war would be greatly impaired and I feel absolutely sure that Bomber Command and the USAAF went a very long way in achieving the collapse of industry within the Third Reich.

Most aircrew believed that the harder they hit Germany the easier it would be for the Allied soldiers in the land battles of Europe and the Red Army on the Eastern Front to overcome German resistance. The bombing offensives ensured that France and the Low Countries would not be turned into the Killing Fields they had been for the Allied soldiers in the First World War. To avoid another bloody massacre of that magnitude was worth all the efforts of Bomber Command.

Historians might never agree as to what were the overall achievements of Bomber Command in their contribution to final victory but most aircrew who fought in the skies over Germany will agree that at the end of the war looking down at the rubble in the bomb-scarred, burned-out cities of Germany that the horrors of war had been brought into the homes of the German people and one could only hope that they would never again embark on such a reign of terror as they had unleashed in Europe from 1939 to 1945. Many of the historians on their deliberations on the Second World War seemed to be generally agreed that the morale of the German civilian population was never broken and that many factories and workshops were still producing at the end of the war. Many of them leave these statements to be accepted or rejected, but in my opinion the morale factor has always needed a little more examination and the questions that are sometimes not easily answered are:

One: Did the faith, trust and adulation that the German people have for Hitler maintain their morale and in the end did they expect him to produce a miracle to save them from defeat?

Two: Was the truth of the matter that the Third Reich was such a police state that anyone who showed any opposition to the party line or showed any sign of weakening under the bombardment was dealt with swiftly by the police or Gestapo and quickly removed from the scene, perhaps in some cases not to be heard of again? In other words was morale maintained by strict policing and a fear of the secret police? In the latter part of the war when defeat was staring Germany in the face and the war was only being continued because of the stupidity of Hitler was morale maintained by promising the people that resistance would be better than surrender and only in their efforts to supply their fighting services could they hope to delay unconditional surrender?

Perhaps it was a combination of all these factors plus others that kept some level of morale, but in my humble opinion I cannot imagine any peoples anywhere in the world not having their morale severely dented by mass bombing like that which had been meted out to the German towns and cities.

I cannot believe that the German soldiers, sailors and airmen were impervious to the letters they were receiving from their homes in the bombed and blasted cities and towns giving them details of their dead and injured relatives and telling them of the utter devastation of their homeland. I am inclined to think that morale under these circumstances must have been hard to maintain both at home and at the front. In contrast to the

German civilian morale there is little doubt that raids by Bomber Command on the German centres of industry boosted the morale of the whole British nation especially the period between the retreat from Dunkirk in June 1940 and the D-Day landings in Normandy on 6th June 1944. On many days during this period the nation had very little to enthuse about, but there were always the bombing raids and the people knew that these were hitting at the heartland of German industry.

The hard-working folks employed in the war factories and workshops turning out the weapons in preparation for the Allied attack on Fortress Europe were cheered by the deeds of Bomber Command. Not only did the raids on Germany cheer the British civilian population but also the many troops training for the Second Front and I am sure helped the morale of Allied troops in Italy and in the Far East. News of the raids broadcast by the BBC would be picked up in the occupied countries to bring them hope for the future. Many of the peoples of the Low Countries and France no doubt heard the bomber force each night as they winged their way overhead en route for Germany and this could only be good for their morale.

There is little doubt that bombing raids affected morale one way or another in Britain, in Germany and the occupied countries, and to some extent must have had a bearing on both Allied and enemy front line troops. Perhaps it had a greater bearing than we are ever likely to discover.

I have read many books and articles written by historians about the bombing offensive carried out by the RAF and the USAAF on Germany in the Second World War and many and varied have been their views. I have found some to be very accurate, others less accurate, some complimentary, others less complimentary and some extremely critical. Some historians have researched their subject well, while others have taken little trouble to find out the overall achievements of this very important contribution to the Allied war effort. The airmen who, since the war, have pointed out to the historians that they thought the bomber offensive was being sold short in the history books were more or less told they were overstating their cases.

However I have noticed as time goes on there appears to be a wind of change in the historians' attitude and much more credit is now being given to the achievements of the bomber offensive. The change of attitude is probably due to the subject having been researched in depth and more and more information becoming available especially over the past ten years.

Like many thousands of other operational aircrew who took part in the bombing of Germany I am proud to have played a part in the defeat of the Third Reich and I have written this book in the hope that it has conveyed to the reader something of my experiences, thoughts and feelings while serving as a bomb aimer on No 76 Halifax Squadron and No 7 Lancaster Pathfinder Squadron. Forty years is a long time ago but I have endeavoured to tell my story from memory and from the many notes I have made throughout the years. I have tried to keep it as accurate and as straightforward as possible so hope my memory has served me well.

It is to be hoped that history books of the future will show this passage of arms to be one of the greatest in the long history of Great Britain, the Commonwealth and Empire, for there is little doubt it should be given a very prominent and honoured place in our country's history.

Appendix

*Halifax Operations carried out while with 76 Squadron
at Linton-on-Ouse and Holme on Spalding Moor, Yorkshire, 1943.*

Target	Date	Role	Target	Date	Role
Dortmund	23/5/43	Main Force	Aachen	13/7/43	Main Force
Düsseldorf	25/5/43	Main Force	Montbelliard	15/7/43	Main Force
Essen	27/5/43	Main Force	Hamburg	29/7/43	Main Force
Wuppertal	29/5/43	Main Force	Remscheid	30/7/43	Main Force
Düsseldorf	11/6/43	Main Force	Hamburg	2/8/43	Main Force
Bochum	12/6/43	Main Force	Mannheim	9/8/43	Main Force
Krefeld	21/6/43	Main Force	Milan (Italy)	12/8/43	Main Force
Mulheim	22/6/43	Main Force	Peenemünde	17/8/43	Main Force
Wuppertal	24/6/43	Main Force	Leverkusen	22/8/43	Main Force
Gelsenkirchen	25/6/43	Main Force	Berlin	23/8/43	Main Force
Cologne	28/6/43	Main Force	Munich	6/9/43	Main Force
Cologne	3/7/43	Main Force	Bochum	29/9/43	Main Force
Gelsenkirchen	9/7/43	Main Force	Kassel	3/10/43	Main Force

All the above sorties were carried out on Halifax bombers and were all night
operations.

*Lancaster Operations carried out while with No 7 PFF Squadron, Oakington during 1944
on Lancaster Bombers.*

Target	Date	Role	Day/Night
Kamen	11/9/44	Visual Backer Up Marker	Day
Munster	12/9/44	VBU Marker	Day
Nordstern	13/9/44	VBU Marker	Day
Boulogne	17/9/44	VBU Marker	Day
Calais	20/9/44	VBU Marker	Day
Neuss Ruhr	23/9/44	VBU Marker	Night
Calais	25/9/44	VBU Marker	Day
Calais	27/9/44	VBU Marker	Day

Bottrop	30/9/44	VBU Marker	Day
Duisberg	14/10/44	VBU Marker	Day
Duisberg	14/10/44	VBU Marker	Night
Wilhelmshaven	15/10/44	VBU Marker	Night
Stuttgart	19/10/44	VBU Marker	Night
Essen	23/10/44	VBU Marker	Night
Essen	25/10/44	VBU Marker	Day
Cologne	28/10/44	VBU Marker	Day
Bochum	4/11/44	VBU Marker	Night
Wanne Eickel	9/11/44	Primary Visual Marker	Day
Dortmund	11/11/44	VBU Marker	Night
Jülich	16/11/44	VBU Marker	Day
Wamme Eickel	18/11/44	VBU Marker	Night
Karlsruhe	4/12/44	VBU Marker	Night
Osnabrück	6/12/44	VBU Marker	Night
Essen	12/12/44	VBU Marker	Night
Duisberg	17/12/44	VBU Marker	Night
Mulheim Essen (A/port)	24/12/44	VBU Marker	Day
Cologne	30/12/44	VBU Marker	Night

Operations carried out with No 7 Pathfinder Force Squadron, Oakington, 1945, on Lancaster Bombers.

Target	Date	Role	Day/Night
Nuremberg	2/1/45	Primary Visual Marker	Night
Hanover	5/1/45	Primary Visual Marker	Night
Hanau	6/1/45	Visual Backer Up Marker	Night
Munich	7/1/45	Visual Backer Up Marker	Night
Dulmen	14/1/45	Visual Backer Up Marker	Night
Cleve	9/2/45	Visual Backer Up Marker	Night
Bohlen	13/2/45	Deputy Master Bomber	Night
Chemnitz	14/2/45	Primary Visual Marker	Night
Worms	21/2/45	Visual Backer Up Marker	Night
Mainz	27/2/45	Deputy Master Bomber	Day
Dessau	7/3/45	Visual Backer Up Marker	Night
Hamburg	8/3/45	Primary Visual Marker	Night
Essen	11/3/45	Deputy Master Bomber	Day
Homberg	14/3/45	Deputy Master Bomber	Night
Recklinghausen	20/3/45	Deputy Master Bomber	Day
Hamburg	31/3/45	Deputy Master Bomber	Day
Harburg	4/4/45	Visual Backer Up Marker	Night
Hamburg	8/4/45	Deputy Master Bomber	Night
Leipzig	10/4/45	Deputy Master Bomber	Day
Kiel	13/4/45	Deputy Master Bomber	Night
Bremen	22/3/45	Primary Visual Marker	Day

Bibliography

Braddon Russell   Cheshire V.C. (Evans 1954)
Bennett D.C.T.   Pathfinder   (Muller 1958)
Chorley W.R.   To see the Dawn Breaking   (W.R. Chorley 1981)
Churchill Winston   The Second World War   (Cassells 1948–54)
Deighton Len   Bomber   (Cape 1970)
Harris Marshal of the RAF   Bomber Offensive   (Collins 1947)
Hastings Max   Bomber Command   (Pan Books Ltd 1981)

Abbreviations Codenames and Technical Terms

A.O.C.	Air Officer Commanding
C.A.S.	Chief of Air Staff
D.R.	Dead Recconing Navigation
E.T.A.	Estimated Time of Arrival
F.I.D.O.	System of burning fuel along sides of runways to clear fog
Flak	Fliegerabwehrkanonen German Anti-Aircraft Gun
Gee	British Radio Navigation Aid first used 1942
H.C.U.	Heavy Conversion Unit
H2S	British Radar Navigation and Blind Bombing Aid fitted to P.F.F. aircraft and other selected aircraft from 1943 onwards
L.M.F.	Lack of moral fibre
Newhaven	Pathfinder code name target marking. Blind by H2S and supported by visual markers
I.T.W.	Initial Training Wing
Oboe	British blind bombing device fitted to Mosquito aircraft of P.F.F. and controlled by transmissions from ground stations
O.T.U.	Operational Training Unit
Paramatta	Pathfinder code name for target marking by blind dropped ground markers (with prefix 'musical' Oboe guided)
P.F.F.	Path Finder Force
R/T	Radio/Telephone i.e. voice communication air to air or air to ground
Wanganui	Pathfinder code name for target marking by blind dropped skymarkers (with prefix 'musical' Oboe guided)
'Window'	Tinfoil strips dropped by allied bombers to confuse German radar
W/T	Wireless transmission. Morse signals

INDEX

Index

193

195